商务馆学汉语辅助读物
世界汉语教学学会审订

An ABC of Chinese Culture
中国文化入门

〔美〕Robert DiYanni　　　Theresa Jen　编著
　　　　　　　　　　　　　　　陈国华　审订

商务印书馆
创于1897　The Commercial Press
2019年·北京

图书在版编目（CIP）数据

中国文化入门／（美）狄亚尼（DiYanni, R.），（美）任（Jen, T.）
编著. —北京：商务印书馆，2009（2019.12重印）
（商务馆学汉语辅助读物）
ISBN 978-7-100-05962-6

I. ①中… II. ①狄…②任… III. ①汉语－对外汉语教学－语言读物
②文化－基本知识－中国－英、汉 IV. ①H195.5 G12

中国版本图书馆CIP数据核字（2008）第137028号

An ABC of Chinese Culture
中国文化入门

〔美〕Robert DiYanni　　Theresa Jen　编著

商 务 印 书 馆 出 版
（北京王府井大街36号 邮政编码 100710）
商 务 印 书 馆 发 行
北京中科印刷有限公司印刷
ISBN 978-7-100-05962-6

2009年12月第1版　　　开本 710×1000 1/16
2019年12月北京第2次印刷　印张 11½
定价：45.00 元

Author Biography

Robert DiYanni is Director of International Services at the College Board. A Professor of English and Humanities at New York University, Dr. DiYanni has lectured and conducted workshops for teachers of English and interdisciplinary humanities in the US, Mexico, Europe, and Asia. He has written and edited more than twenty-five books, including *The McGraw-Hill Book of Poetry, The McGraw-Hill Book of Fiction, The Scribner Handbook for Writers, Writing about the Humanities, Literature: An Introduction,* and *Modern American Prose.*

Dr. Theresa Jen is Associate Director of International Services at the College Board and Director & Professor at the Wharton School, University of Pennsylvania. She is also a consultant to ETS (Educational Testing Services) and ACTFL (American Council on the Teaching of Foreign Languages). A renowned scholar with prominent leadership, Dr. Jen has been active in both international and American mainstream educational fields. She has been invited as a keynote speaker in numerous national and international conferences. She has also lectured and conducted English and teacher training workshops in the US, Europe, and Asia.

目 录
Catalogue

Preface

We wrote *An ABC of Chinese Culture* to introduce readers to basic aspects of Chinese cultural life. Our goal has been to provide brief overviews of key cultural concepts in entries that can be read quickly, yet are long enough to provide useful basic information. Each of the topics we have included can be read and digested in a few minutes, making *An ABC of Chinese Culture* a handy first guide for those who need a quick and easily accessible reference to things Chinese. **The book is designed not as a scholarly resource, but as a first acquaintance with basic concepts of Chinese culture. Readers who know little or nothing of Chinese culture, but who have an interest can begin with *An ABC of Chinese Culture* and then proceed to more detailed and scholarly works, some examples of which are provided at the end of this book.**

We organized the book alphabetically (in English) to make the topics easy to find. We have also highlighted with bold print in each entry words linked to other entries in the book. Thus in the discussion of Confucius, the word **Analects** is bolded to indicate that there is an entry on his Analects, and in the discussions of Tang dynasty poets Du Fu and Li Bai, the word **Tang** is bolded to indicate an entry on the Tang dynasty.

The book was written in English and translated into Chinese, which makes it accessible to those knowing either language. It can also be used by those who know either language and are studying the other by reading for comprehension in the new target language.

An ABC of Chinese Culture should be useful to visitors to China, but certainly not restricted to those visitors. We hope that the book proves useful as well to those outside of China who would like to make a start learning about the many fascinating aspects and elements of one of the world's oldest and greatest cultures.

It is also our hope that readers of *An ABC of Chinese Culture* will follow up these brief introductory essays with further reading in the many fascinating books about China, its people, its history, and its culture.

前　言

　　我们写《中国文化入门》的目的是向读者介绍中国文化生活的一些基本方面。以简短易读而又足以提供有用的基本信息的章目，为读者提供重点文化概念的纵观，一直是我们的目标。我们收录的每一个话题读者都可以在几分钟之内看完并领会，这一点使得《中国文化入门》对于那些需要快速方便地查阅参考中国知识的人来说，成了一本好用的首选的指导书。**本书不是作为一个学术资源而设计的，而是对中国文化的基本概念的一个初步介绍。对中国文化知之甚少或一无所知，但有兴趣了解的读者，可以读《中国文化入门》作为开端，然后进一步读更详细的学术著作。本书结尾提供了这样的一些学术著作的书目。**

　　本书按字母顺序（英文的）编排，这样读者容易找到话题。我们用粗体字凸显了在一个章目里与本书其他章目有关联的词。因此，在讲《孔子》时，《论语》一词用粗体以显示关于孔子的《论语》本书有一个章目；在讲唐代诗人杜甫和李白时，唐字用粗体以显示关于唐朝本书有一个章目。

　　本书用英语写成，又译成汉语，这样可以使只懂英语或只懂汉语的人阅读。只懂英语，正在学习汉语的人，或只懂汉语，正在学习英语的人，可以用此书通过目标语阅读以获得理解。

　　对于到中国旅游的人，当然不仅限于对这些游客，《中国文化入门》应该很有用。我们希望本书也会对这样一些人有用：他们不在中国，但愿意尝试了解中国文化（世界上最悠久最伟大的文化之一）的很多迷人的方面和元素。

　　我们也希望《中国文化入门》的读者们会读完这些简短的介绍性文章之后进一步读一些关于中国、中国人、中国历史和中国文化的好书。

Acupuncture

Acupuncture has been practiced in China for more than two thousand years. It is a therapy that involves inserting thin sterile needles into the body at a series of strategically designated "acupuncture points", and manipulating them in order to restore human health. According to Chinese medical theory, a person's health is contingent upon having an uninterrupted flow of *Qi*, or energy, along a system of channels or pathways within the human body. When the flow of *Qi* is interrupted, unhealthy symptoms appear, which is the goal of acupuncture to eliminate.

The needles are inserted and vibrated in order to stimulate nerve impulses along the body's natural channels through which a person's *Qi* flows. The *Qi* flows through three **Yin** and three **Yang** channels of a person's two hands and feet, making twelve central channels in all. For each channel there is an internal and an external pathway. The superficial external pathway is the set of points and lines typically shown on an acupuncture chart like the one shown here. The deep internal pathway follows the course of the body cavities.

In Chinese medical theory acupuncture is designed to normalize and regulate the balance of *Qi*, or vital energy throughout the body. Such a theory is in accord with general Chinese philosophical principles of **Confucianism**, which argues for balance and harmony in social life, and of **Daoism,** which postulates the goal of living in balance and harmony with nature.

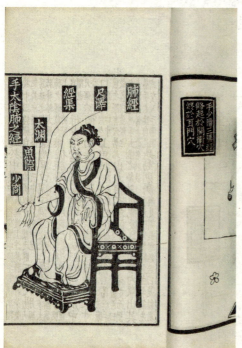

一本古代的针灸图书

针　刺

　　针刺在中国已有两千多年的历史。它是将细长的无菌针刺入人体的一系列特定部位（即穴位），用一定的技法对针进行操控，以使人恢复身体健康的一种治疗手段。中医理论认为，人体健康依赖于体内的气（即一种能量）沿着经络不断流动。一旦气受阻，就会出现各种不健康症状。针刺可以打通阻塞，消除症状。

　　针刺入穴位后，通过搓捻或提插，对穴位加以刺激，产生神经脉冲（酸、麻、热、胀等感觉），脉冲沿经脉传导，气也就顺着经脉流通。人的双手和双足各有三条**阴**脉和三条**阳**脉，这样一共有十二条经脉。每一条经脉有内外通道连接脏腑和肢节。经脉的表层外通道就是右面这幅针灸穴位图所显示的一系列穴位和经络，深层内通道则通往体内被称为脏腑的各个空腔。

　　在中医理论里，实施针刺是为了调节和恢复人体内气的平衡。这一理论符合提倡社会生活平衡与和谐的中国**儒家**哲学思想以及追求人与自然和谐相处的**道家**思想。

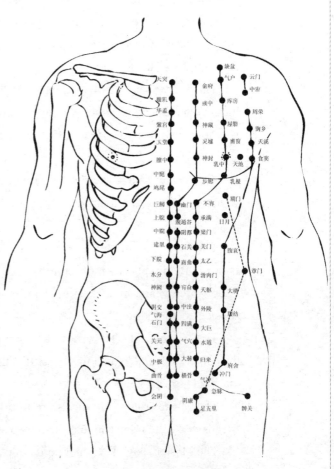

人体穴位图（李杨桦绘）

Analects

Confucius' wisdom has been compiled by his students in a book entitled the *Analects* (Lun Yu). Soon after his death, Confucius's sayings and those of his followers were gathered together to compile the *Analects*. Referred to in the *Analects* as the "Master", Confucius emphasizes the duties and obligations of the individual as a member of society, focusing frequently on proper forms of human conduct. Here are a few samples of the Master's wisdom.

The Master said, "Is it not a pleasure, having learned something, to try it out at due intervals? Is it not a joy to have friends come from afar? And, is it not gentlemanly not to take offence when others fail to recognize your abilities?"

The Master said, "The rule of virtue can be compared to the Pole Star which commands the homage of the multitude of stars without leaving its place."

The Master said, "Observe what a man has in mind to do when his father is living, and then observe what he does when his father is dead. If, for three years, he makes no changes to his father's ways, he can be considered a good son."

The Master said, "The virtue of the prince is like the wind; the virtue of the common people is like the grass. It is the nature of grass to bend when the wind blows upon it."

The Master said, "My ideals are to bring comfort to the old, to have friends that I can trust, and to cherish the young."

The Master said, "I was not born with knowledge; I am one who loves antiquity and who avidly seeks understanding there."

《论　语》

孔子像

　　孔子的智慧被他的弟子追记并编纂成书，取名为《论语》。孔子死后不久，他和他一些弟子的言行便被收集起来，编成《论语》。书中孔子被尊称为"子"，他强调个人作为社会一员所承担的责任和义务，经常教导人们在言语举止上要符合礼。以下是孔子的部分智慧言语：

　　子曰："学而时习之，不亦说乎？有朋自远方来，不亦乐乎？人不知而不愠，不亦君子乎？"

　　子曰："为政以德。譬如北辰，居其所而众星共之。"

　　子曰："父在，观其志；父殁，观其行；三年无改於父之道，可谓孝矣。"

　　子曰："君子之德风，小人之德草，草上之风必偃。"

　　子曰："老者安之，朋友信之，少者怀之。"

　　子曰："我非生而知之者；好古，敏以求之者也。"

孔子讲学图

Ancestor Worship

To worship their ancestors people offer sacrifices to their ancestors regularly, based on the belief that the dead have a soul existing, remain involved in their family's affairs, and influence the fortunes of the living. The goal of ancestor worship is twofold: (1) to honor one's ancestors and ensure their well-being; (2) to encourage their positive disposition, particularly when seeking realization of one's wishes or needing help. The dead can bring prosperity and good fortune, but if neglected by their descendants, the ancestors can become "hungry ghosts", both dangerous and destructive, as they are cut adrift in the

安徽胡氏宗祠（戴军明摄影）

spirit world.

Among the most common ritual aspects of ancestor worship are making offerings to provide for the ancestor's well-being after life. These offerings may be practical objects such as a comb or toothbrush, articles of clothing, food and liquor, etc. Some items that the ancestor often used and appreciated when alive are often placed in the coffin as burial artifacts and it is laid to rest, since people believe that in the other world, the dead can still use the stuff that they used when alive. After the funeral, offerings continue, and may include luxury items, including favorite foods and wines, and symbolic "spirit" money, which is placed in bowls on the ancestral altar, or burned with incense.

The family altar, before which such offerings are placed, typically includes a portrait or photograph and a commemorative plaque, along with cups or bowls for the offerings. The altar for a recently deceased relative is kept up for forty-nine days. Once the altar is dismantled, ancestral tablets take its place, as the ancestors are imagined to dwell in such commemorative tablets, which are kept in a small home shrine or in a family ancestral temple. Incense is lit before the tablets, ideally each day, and food and other offerings may be made a few times a month.

Ancestor worship remains an important part of the belief system of many Chinese people today. It reflects, in consummate form, the **Confucian** ideal of filial piety.

祖先崇拜

　　人们崇拜祖先，定期举行祭祀，因为他们相信死者有灵魂存在，能够继续参与家庭事务，并影响活人的命运。祖先崇拜有两个目的：一是向先人表达崇敬之情，确保他们在阴间能过得好；二是祈求他们的保佑，特别是在自己希望达成某种愿望或需要帮助之时。祖先可以给后人带来繁荣和好运，但如果受到后人的忽视，祖先则可能变为危险的和具有破坏力的"饿鬼"或"恶鬼"游荡在阴间。

　　祖先崇拜的仪式里最常见的是提供祭品，以满足祖先在阴间生活的需要。祭品可以是实用物品，如梳子或牙刷、衣物、食品和酒水等。下葬时，一些祖先在世时常用和喜爱的物品常被放在棺材里作为陪葬品，

祠堂中摆放着祖宗牌位（刘国辉摄影）

年俗·祭祖（李金鹏摄影）

因为人们相信死者到了阴间还能继续使用生前所用过的东西。葬礼完毕后继续祭供，祭品可能是一些奢侈品，包括死者生前喜好的食物和酒，还有象征性的冥钱，摆放在灵台前或与香火一起烧掉。

摆放祭品的灵台上通常有死者的一幅画像或照片和一个纪念牌，还有用来盛放祭品的杯子或碗碟。为刚去世的亲人设的灵台保留四十九天。灵台拆除后，祖先牌位取而代之，人们想象亡灵就在这牌位之中。牌位放置在家庭的小神龛里或者祠堂里。灵位前供着香火，最好香火不断，而且食物和其他祭品可能每月供奉数次。

祖先崇拜今天仍是很多中国人信仰体系的重要组成部分，它集中体现了**儒家**的孝道。

Bamboo

In Chinese culture, bamboo is held in the highest esteem, along with the chrysanthemum, the ume blossom (commonly translated as plum blossom), and the orchid. These "four of great nobility" represent four particular aspects of a noble person's character. Bamboo is associated with perseverance. Bamboo blossoms only once every sixty to eighty years and dies shortly after. Its long life makes it a symbol of longevity.

Bamboo is a hard wood as well as a hardy one. It is light and exceptionally strong, and thus lends itself to a wide variety of uses, including bridges, fences, flooring, furniture, houses, kites, scaffolding, toys, walking sticks, weapons, and ancient writing strips. The staple food of the **Giant Panda**, bamboo has long been a cultural icon in China. Bamboo plants, the pine and the plum tree are known as "the three friends in winter".

The residence of the famous **Tang dynasty** poet, **Du Fu**, was situated among a luxuriant growth of bamboo. Du Fu and many other Chinese poets refering often to bamboo in their poems, as the ancient Chinese literati, both poets and painters, had the deepest regard for the plant. Among the many important Chinese painters, the one best known for his paintings of bamboo is Zheng Banqiao (1693 — 1765) in the **Qing dynasty**. Among the many poems he composed about bamboo, he wrote these lines: "Orchids collect in remote mountain precipices, bamboos sway to make cool shade. With the vault of heaven serving as a big room, I lie down among them in a light spirit."

清代的竹衣（徽州文化博物馆供）

竹

在中国文化中，竹与菊花、梅花、兰花一起享有极高的地位，这"四君子"代表一个高贵之人的四种品质。竹常与坚韧不拔的意志联系在一起。它每六十到八十年开花一次，此后不久便会死去。因其生长期长，竹成为长寿的象征。

竹子是一种坚韧而耐寒的植物，质轻但特别结实。它用途广泛，可用来建桥、做栅栏、制地板、造家具、盖房屋、做风筝、搭脚手架、制作玩具、拐杖、武器和古时书写用的竹简。竹还是**大熊猫**的主要食物。在中国，竹长期以来就是一种文化符号，它与松、梅一起被称为"岁寒三友"。

唐朝著名诗人**杜甫**的家便位于一片茂密的竹林之中。杜甫和很多其他中国诗人都常常在诗中提到竹。中国文人，包括诗人和画家，都对竹有着极深的感情。在众多中国重要的画家中，**清朝**的郑板桥（1693 — 1765）尤以画竹出名。他写过很多关于竹的诗，其中一首是：

> 高山峻壁见芝兰，
> 竹影遮斜几片寒。
> 便以乾坤为巨室，
> 老夫高枕卧其间。

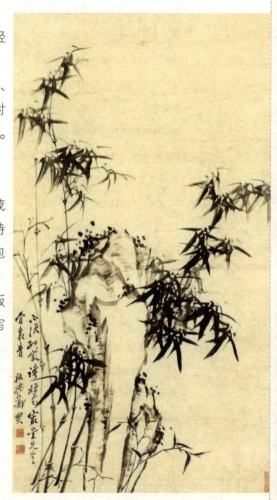

清·郑板桥《墨竹图》

Book of Songs

Chinese literature begins with the *Book of Songs*, called the Odes for short. It is an anthology of songs, poems, and hymns which date from the West **Zhou dynasty** (1046 BC – 771 BC) to the middle of the Spring and Autumn Period (770 BC – 476 BC). The poems, which were collected from the areas which include central and northern China, cover a wide range of subjects, reflecting the life in central and nothern China at the time. They include poems about affairs of state and about political and military matters, as well as poems about the experiences of people from all social classes and all walks of life. The poems in the *Book of Songs* make mention of numerous plants, and animals; they are a repository of information about nature and also about musical instruments, food, clothing, buildings, and military equipment.

Considered one of the *Five Classics* identified during the **Han dynasty** (206 BC – AD 220), the 305 poems of the *Book of Songs* are believed to have been selected by **Confucius** from nearly ten times that number. Of these, 160 are folk songs; 74 minor odes, sung at court festivities; 31 major odes, sung at court ceremonies; and 40 hymns, sung on sacrificial occasions.

Confucius referred to the *Book of Songs*, or the *Odes*, frequently in his *Analects*, citing them as essential knowledge for the scholar and gentleman. Here is a brief poem that describes a situation common to people from all social classes:

By the willows of the Eastern Gate, whose leaves are so thick, at dusk we were to meet; And now the evening star is bright.

By the willows of the Eastern Gate, whose leaves are so close, at dusk we were to meet; And now the evening star is pale.

《诗　经》

中国文学始于《诗经》(简称《诗》)。《诗经》是一部诗歌集，所收录的诗歌创作于西周(前 1046 — 前 771)到春秋(前 770 — 前 476)中期这一阶段。这些诗歌收集自中国中部和北部地区，题材丰富，反映了当时中国中部和北部各地人民的生活。这些诗有的涉及政治、军事等国家大事，有的描述了社会各阶层、各行业人们的经历和体验。《诗经》中的诗提到无数植物、动物名称，记载了关于自然的丰富信息，还提到各种乐器、食品、服装、建筑和军事装备。

汉朝(前 206 — 220)将《诗经》列为《五经》之一，其 305 首诗据说是**孔子**从近三千首中挑选出来的，其中属于民谣的《国风》160 首；在宫廷节日上演唱的《小雅》74 首；在隆重宫廷典礼上演唱的《大雅》31 首；在祭祀活动上演唱的《颂》40 首。

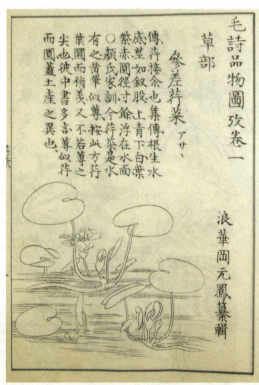

《毛诗品物图考》书影

孔子在《**论语**》中经常提到《诗经》或《诗》，认为这是学者和君子应掌握的基本知识。下面这首短诗描述了对各阶层人来说都很普通的一个场景：

> 东门之杨，其叶牂牂。
>
> 昏以为期，明星煌煌。
>
> 东门之杨，其叶肺肺。
>
> 昏以为期，明星晢晢。

Buddhism

Of the three most important Chinese religious philosophies – Buddhism, Confucianism, and Daoism – Buddhism is the one that is not home-grown. Buddhism came to China from India during the **Han dynasty** (206 BC – AD 220). Its influence on Chinese culture has been considerable, and Chinese culture in return has had a significant influence on Buddhism, with mutual influences on politics, culture, literature, and philosophy, for more than two thousand years.

Because Buddhism originated in India, a country with very different religious and cultural traditions, Buddhism underwent some degree of transformation in China. It was merged into Chinese traditions such as **ancestor worship**, respect for elders, and the Chinese rather than the Hindu hierarchical system.

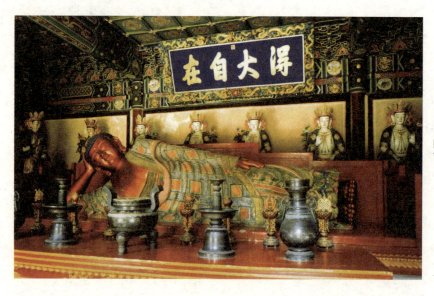

卧佛

Buddhism began to gain popularity in China after the fall of the Han dynasty. Buddhist missionaries from India and central Asia spread the Buddhist philosophy and provided a strong stimulus for trade in objects both ordinary and valuable associated with the religion. Jewels and precious metals, for example, were needed as decoration for Buddhist images and temples.

The essence of Buddhist teaching is encapsulated in the four noble truths: (1) life is suffering; (2) the cause of this suffering is selfish desire; (3) suffering can only end with the elimination of selfish desire; (4) and the method for achieving the end of suffering is by following the eight-fold path, which centers on meditation, morality, and discipline, as the path to enlightenment. In China, these ideals are placed in the context of compassion, idealized in the Bodhisattva, who defers his own entry into nirvana to help others.

杭州灵隐寺烧香的善男信女

佛　教

在中国，释、儒、道是三个最重要的宗教哲学派别，其中只有释（即佛教）不是本土产生的。佛教于**汉朝**（前 206 — 220）从印度传入中国。此后两千多年里，佛教对中国文化产生了相当大的影响，而中国文化对佛教也有重大影响，二者在政治、文化、文学和哲学方面相互作用和融合，最终使佛教成为中国文化的一部分。

由于佛教发源地印度有着和中国完全不同的宗教和文化传统，佛教传入中国后经过了一定程度的改造，与**祖先崇拜**、尊敬长者等中国传统以及中国的而不是印度的等级制度相融合。

佛教于**汉朝**末年开始在中国流行。来自印度和中亚的佛教僧侣四处传播佛教思想，同时也推动了与佛教相关的普通和贵重物品贸易的发展，例如建造佛像和寺庙所需的珠宝和贵重金属。

佛教教义的精华浓缩在"四谛"（即四条真理）中：一为"苦谛"，即把人生判定为痛苦，全无幸福欢乐可言；二为"集谛"，即造成痛苦的原因是私欲；三为"灭谛"，即只有通过涅槃，也就是消灭私欲，才能结束痛苦；四

浙江普陀山《南海观音像》

为"道谛"，即只有遵从强调"慧、戒、定"的"八正道"才能从痛苦中解脱出来。在中国，这些理想与慈悲联系在一起。人们视菩萨为慈悲的化身。菩萨推迟自己的涅槃以普渡众生。

唐代壁画《观世音像》

Calligraphy

Calligraphy, or beautiful writing, is at the heart of the higher forms of Chinese culture. One of the three perfections or gentlemanly arts, calligraphy is linked with its companion arts of poetry and painting. All three – poetry, painting, and calligraphy – were considered aspects of the same art since poems were written in calligraphy and paintings were typically accompanied by such calligraphied poems.

地球墨（徽州文化博物馆供）

Unlike in the west, where calligraphy is considered a minor art, in China the art of calligraphy has long enjoyed a high status among the arts. People believe that the style in which a person writes can communicate something essential about him or her. In recording the movements of hand, wrist, and arm, the calligraphy brush acts like a kind of seismograph, the brush is more than a mere tool with a utilitarian purpose. Because writing and calligraphy are held in such high esteem, the brushes used in their creation are highly valued, with some considered works of art in their own right, much as a violin bow might be so considered.

Because the brush is wielded by the artist /calligrapher, it is considered a living extension, a part of the artist /calligrapher's body, which conveys the imprint of his mind and heart. In producing calligraphy according to the ancient rules and guidelines, the writer reveals his character and spirit as well as his intentions. As such, the quality of a poem depends as much on how it is written as on what is written – on how it is calligraphied onto the paper as much as on its content.

各种各样的毛笔（毛尧泉摄影）

书 法

　　书法位居中华文化高层形式的核心，是三种高雅艺术之一，常与诗歌和绘画艺术联系在一起。诗歌、绘画和书法被视为同一艺术的三个方面，因为诗歌需要通过书法写下来，而绘画上通常配有书法优美的诗。

　　西方人认为书法只是一门小艺术；在中国，书法艺术却一向在各类艺术中享有崇高的地位。"字如其人"、"书为心画"，人们相信一个人的字可以传达他的一些本质的东西。毛笔记录手、手腕和手臂的运动，就像地震仪记录地震一样，因此毛笔不仅是一种实用工具。由于书法地位崇高，用于创作书法作品的毛笔也就很珍贵，有的毛笔本身就被视为艺术品，就像西方人眼中小提琴的琴弓一样。

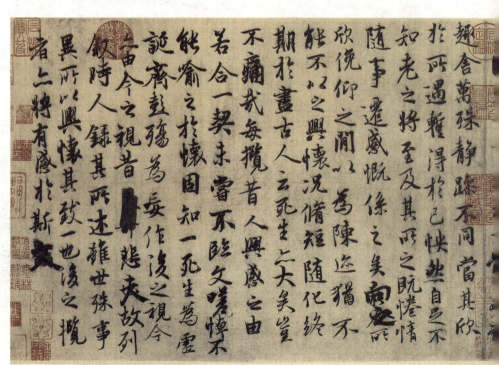

王羲之《兰亭集序》

明代的砚（徽州文化博物馆供）

　　艺术家、书法家作画写字需要挥笔，因此毛笔被视为有灵性之物，是艺术家、书法家身体的延伸，能传达他们的思想和情感。作者在按照古老的规则创作书法作品时，会流露出他的品性、精神和意图。因此，一首诗的好坏不仅在于它写了什么，还在于它是如何写的，也就是说，对于一首诗，写这首诗的书法和这首诗的内容同样重要。

Confucius

Confucius (Kong Qiu, Master Kong) is the best known and the most important of Chinese sages. Confucius lived from 551 to 479 BC, a time of political turmoil. Confucius was a great scholar, a master of the traditional wisdom of Chinese thought as collected in **Analects**. His most important legacy was, however, as an educator rather than as an official, which he was for a time.

Confucius was a pragmatic thinker who focused on this world rather than on the next one. Unlike the more mystical **Laotze**, the originator of **Daoism** who turned inward, Confucius looked outward toward society. Through his teachings recorded in the *Analects,* Confucius emphasized the importance of the traditional values of self-control, propriety, and filial piety. With these virtues in stock, Confucius believed that anarchy could be overcome and social cohesion restored.

Confucius argued that if each individual would be virtuous, the family would live in harmony; if each family lived in harmony, the village would then be harmonious. Village harmony, in turn, would lead to a country focused on moral values that would allow life to be lived in peace to its fullest potential. At the heart of Confucian thought is the concept of "*li*", or propriety, which involves due and proper respect for established forms of conduct. These include good manners, courtesy, politeness, and respect for age. Li is complemented by "*yi*", or duty, a sense of obligation that one has to others. Ultimately and fundamentally, Confucius justified the value of moral behavior by an appeal to experience. His teachings were designed to help people become better individuals and to live improved communal lives on earth. Confucius remains the quintessential Chinese sage.

孔　子

宋·马远《孔子像》

孔子（孔丘，尊称孔夫子）是中国最著名、最重要的圣人。孔子生于公元前551年，卒于公元前479年，生活在一个政治动荡的年代。孔夫子是一位大学者，是中国传统文化思想的集大成者。他的思想集中体现在《论语》中。他虽然当过官，但留给后世最宝贵的遗产却不是他的政绩，而是他的教育思想。

孔子是一位务实的思想家，他注重今生今世，而非来生来世。与**道家**创始人**老子**关注内心世界不同，孔子关注外部社会。《**论语**》中记录的孔子的教导强调克己、复礼和孝道等传统品德的重要性。他认为，人们只要具备了这些品德，混乱状态就会结束，就可以重建和谐稳定的社会。

孔子宣称，如果每一个人都有德，家庭就会和睦；如果每个家庭都和睦，整个村庄就会和谐；村庄和谐，国家必会成为一个重视道德品质的国家，在这样的国家里，人们才能安居乐业，发挥最大的潜能。孔子思想的核心是"礼"，这涉及对行为规范的尊重和遵守。"礼"涵盖礼仪、谦恭、礼貌、敬老。"义"是对"礼"的补充，是对他人的一种责任感。孔子通过唤起人们的亲身体验最终并且在根本上论证了道德行为的价值。他的那些教导是为了助人向善，使大家更和谐地集体生活在世上。孔子至今仍是最具中国本质特征的圣人。

Cuisine

Chinese cuisine is world famous. Every major city in the world offers a wide variety of Chinese food, cooked in a wide range of styles. However, to gain a true appreciation of the marvels and subtle nuances of Chinese cuisine, one has to experience the epicurean gustatory pleasures in China.

The delights of Chinese cuisine have a long history, with each dynasty contributing new recipes, perhaps reaching their peak during the **Qing dynasty** (1616 – 1911). An example of a dish is **Peking Duck,** which was introduced from among the people to the imperial court when it was refined by the court's imperial cook and then returned to the people. Following the imperial dishes are those of the Mansion style of cooking, so named because this cuisine derives from chefs who cooked for the nobility in their mansions. Some cuisines developed for religious and medical reasons, and so there are monastic and therapeutic styles of cooking, with the monastic dishes typically vegetarian and the therapeutic including medicinal herbs and spices. In addition to these ways of designating various Chinese cooking, China's cuisines are also classified geographically according to regions, yielding, for example, the four major regional cooking styles: Cantonese, Shandong, Sichuan, and Huaiyang.

Two additional things might be mentioned about Chinese cuisine. One is the role courtesy and culture play in serving and consuming a Chinese meal. Respect for others, especially for elders, is considered essential, whether dining at home or in public. Another is the importance of chopsticks, whose use forms an essential aspect of the experience of Chinese cuisine. The conventions regarding proper use of chopsticks are a small-scale but no less important aspect of Chinese cuisine culture than those regulating the observance of social proprieties.

烹 饪

中餐世界闻名。全世界每一个大城市都向人们提供形式多样、口味各异的中餐。但是，要想真正了解中餐的精妙之处，人们仍须亲自到中国当一回美食家。

美味的中餐历史源远流长，各朝各代新的菜肴层出不穷。**清朝**（1616—1911）也许是中国烹饪的鼎盛时期。**北**

川菜

京烤鸭便是从民间传入宫廷，经宫廷御厨改良后又传至民间的一道有名的菜肴。除宫廷菜外还有官府菜，这些菜式是由达官贵族府第里的厨师烹制，因而得名。有些菜式则起源于宗教或医药，因此又有斋饭和药膳。斋饭一般为素食，药膳里则常加入中草药和香料。此外，中餐还可以根据地域分为多个派系，如粤菜、鲁菜、川菜和淮扬菜就被合称为"四大菜系"。

关于中餐或许还应注意两点。一是礼貌和文化在上餐与用餐中的作用。不论在家还是在外用餐，都须尊重他人，特别是长者。二是筷子的重要性。使用筷子有一些讲究，这些讲究虽属于细枝末节，但却是中国饮食文化的一个重要方面，不亚于对社交礼节的讲究。

清代公主用的餐具

Daoism

Like **Confucianism**, Daoism (Taoism) is concerned principally with moral and ethical behavior, and is thus more often considered a spiritual philosophy than a religion. Its founder was **Laotze**, about whom little is known, except that he composed the *Daodejing (Tao Te Ching)*, which is usually translated as "The Way and Its Power".

The *Daodejing* summarizes the Daoist philosophy. The Dao (Tao) is the ultimate reality behind existence, a transcendent and eternal spiritual

道教名山 —— 四川青城山（王　晖摄影）

essence. Mysterious and mystical, it is finally incomprehensible and ineffable. As an early section notes: "The Dao that can be described is not the real Dao." In addition, Laotze says: "Those who know don't say, and those who say don't really know." In this sense, the Dao is the governing order of life represented by the rhythm of nature. Daoism is a way of ordering one's life. It is a set of principles used to achieve peace and harmony with the created world.

A central Daoist concept is *te*, which means "virtue" or "power". In Daoism, the *te* of a thing is its essential virtue, identity, integrity. The *te* of a person is his or her genuineness, one's authentic self. One expresses *te* through humility and cooperation and patient attentiveness, rather than through competition and willfulness. The Daoist ideal is one of simplicity and naturalness, indicated by their ideal of *pu*, or "unpainted wood". The Daoist thus prefers the unvarnished natural state, leaving gilt and lacquer to the Confucians. Daoist painting, similarly, uses few and simple lines, suggesting much in little, with human figures in Daoist art kept small in relation to the vastness of nature.

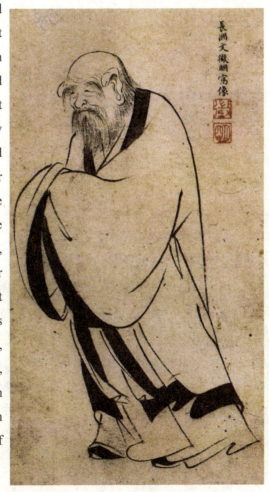

明 · 文徵明《老子像》

道　家

道家和**儒家**一样，其学说主要是关于道德和伦理行为的，因此多被当成一门精神哲学而非宗教。人们对道教的创始人**老子**所知甚少，只知道他创作了《道德经》。

《道德经》集中记录了道家的哲学思想。"道"是隐匿于存在背后的终极现实，是一种超凡、永恒的精神本质。它神秘莫测，永远不可理解和说清。《道德经》开篇就写道："道可道，非常道。"老子还说："知者不言。言者不知。"道无所不在，存在于四季轮回、滔滔江水和鸟鸣百啭中。在此意义上说，道乃是自然节律所代表的生命法则，是人生处世之道，是达到与大千世界和睦、和谐相处的一套原则。

道家学说的一个中心思想是德。道家认为，德是事物的本质、德性和整体。一个人的德是他的真实自我。人通过谦卑、合作和耐心、专注来展现德，而非通过竞争和一意孤行。道家崇尚"朴"（即未上漆的木头）所代表的简单和自然，喜欢未经修饰的自然状态，把镀金和漆绘留给儒家。同样，道家的绘画作品都是用寥寥数笔勾勒而成，以少寓多，道家艺术中，人物形象在广大的自然界中被画得很小。

《老子与道家》书影

老子

道可道非常道名可名非常名無名天地之始有名萬物之母常無欲以觀其妙常有欲以觀其徼此兩者同出而異名同謂之玄玄之又玄眾妙之門天下皆知美之為美斯惡已皆知善之為善斯不善已故有無之相生難易之相成長短之相形高

唐·赵孟頫书法《道德经》

Dragons

Many cultures include dragons among their myths and legends. China is no exception. In fact, Chinese culture has been considered a "dragon culture", one whose people consider themselves "descendents of the dragon", as early Chinese peoples adopted the dragon as their guardian deity. A combination of various animals, including the snake, lizard, alligator, and other reptiles with scales, the dragon later acquired the attributes of other animals, such as the antlers of the deer and the claws of the eagle. Known for its ferocity and its power, the dragon's many powers include its ability to control rainfall, with the kings of the water dragons inhabiting dragon palaces beneath the world's oceans.

北京北海公园的九龙壁

The dragon is associated with the **emperor**. Thus we have the "dragon seat" for the Emperor's throne, "dragon robes" for his attire, and also "dragon beds" and "dragon screens". Dragons form a principal decorative element on buildings, clothing, and articles used initially only by the emperor, but now in modern times, by people from all social ranks and all walks of life. Dragons appeared in various forms throughout the emperor's palace, entwined, for example in columns and embedded in decorative monumental outdoor stone slabs.

Dragons play a significant role in various Chinese **Festivals**, particularly the Dragon Boat Festival, an important holiday in China with a long history. The central event of the festival is a race among boats shaped like dragons, with a dragon head at the prow, and which race to the beat of a drum. One of many other ways dragons feature in Chinese culture is the dragon dance, which is a staple of celebrations during the Chinese **Spring Festival**.

九龙壁局部

龙

　　龙出现在多种文化的神话传说中，中国也不例外。事实上，中国文化一直被视为龙文化，而中国人把自己视为龙的传人，因为古代中国人把龙当成自己的守护神。龙最初呈现出多种动物形象，包括蛇、蜥蜴、鳄鱼和其他带鳞的爬行动物，后来又获得了其他动物的属性特征，如鹿角和鹰爪。龙性情凶猛，法力无穷，龙王住在海底的龙宫里，能呼风唤雨。

　　龙总与**皇帝**联系在一起。皇帝的御座称为"龙椅"，皇帝的服装称为"龙袍"，还有"龙床"、"龙壁"等。龙开始只是皇帝所用的建筑、服饰和物品上的主要装饰成分，不过现在社会各阶层、各行业的人都用。皇宫里，各种形式的龙随处可见，或盘绕在立柱上，或嵌于云龙阶石中。

公园里花草搭建的书法作品《龙》

　　龙在各种中国**节日**，特别是端午节里，扮演重要角色。端午节是中国一个有着悠久历史的重要节日，以赛龙舟为主要庆祝节目。龙舟模仿龙的造型，船头饰有龙头。比赛时，人们随着鼓声划动船桨前进。龙在中国文化中以许多方式出现，其中之一就是舞龙，舞龙是中国**春节**的一项主要庆祝活动。

绣有龙的丝绸睡袍

Du Fu

Du Fu (Tu Fu) (712 – 770) is generally considered one of China's greatest poets, along with **Li Bai** (Li Po), with whom he is often connected. Like Li Bai, Du Fu lived during the **Tang dynasty**'s classical age, the period of China's greatest artistic efflorescence.

Du Fu was considered a "poet-sage" and his poems "poem history". The core of his mind was a concern of the social reality, people's livelihood and sufferings, and his poems recorded faithfully the turmoil of the country and the tribulation of the people, giving sincere sympathy to the persecuted. His poem about "An Lushan and Shi Siming's Rebellion" transcend their historical circumstances, giving voice to the thoughts and feelings, and especially the sufferings and hardships endured by ordinary people in wartime chaos.

Du Fu's poems range widely in subject and form and are written in a variety of styles that capture different social, literary, and linguistic registers. Among his most affecting poems are those that capture the feelings of loss and separation, as does the following famous poem, "Moonlit Night", written in the *lu shi* "regulated eight-line verse" form, which Du Fu used for nearly two thirds of his 1 500 surviving poems.

> *Moonlit Night*
> *In Fuzhou tonight, my wife watches*
> *The moon, alone, and my thoughts*
> *Turn to sadness for our children,*
> *Who don't know why she misses Chang-an.*

Her soft hair is damp with fragrant mist.
Clear light shines, and her arms feel the chill.
When will we lean together in the moonlight
And dry the tears we have shed so long?

Du Fu's fame in China equals that of Shakespeare in the English-speaking world. He exerts great influence on his Chinese poetic successors, and also in Japan he has long been revered, and his influence remains extensive.

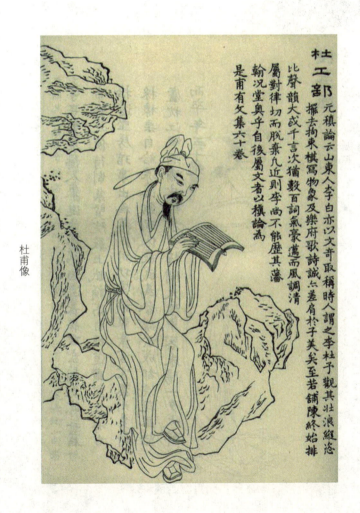

杜甫像

杜 甫

杜甫像

杜甫（712 — 770）与**李白**被公认为中国最伟大的诗人之一，人们常把他们两个相提并论。和李白一样，杜甫生活在中国艺术全盛时期的**唐朝**。

杜甫被尊称为"诗圣"，他的诗被尊称为"诗史"。他的思想的核心是关注社会现实，关心民生疾苦。他的诗忠实地记录了国家的变乱和人民的苦难，对受迫害者寄予了深挚的同情。他描写"安史之乱"的诗歌超越了历史事件本身，抒发了普通百姓的思想与情感，特别是刻画了他们在战乱中所遭受的痛苦和磨难。

杜甫的诗歌题材广泛，形式多变，风格各异，捕捉和记录了不同的社会阶层、文学类别和语言种类。他最感人的诗描写的是生离死别之情。下面这首著名的诗《月夜》就是其中之一。这是一首律诗，在杜甫现存 1 500 首诗中，有近三分之二都是律诗。

月 夜

今夜鄜州月，闺中只独看。

遥怜小儿女，未解忆长安。

香雾云鬟湿，清辉玉臂寒。

何时倚虚幌，双照泪痕干。

杜甫在中国享有极高的声誉，就如同莎士比亚在英语世界的地位一样。他不仅对后代的中国诗人产生了重要的影响，还对日本的诗歌发展产生了广泛影响，在日本一直受到敬仰。

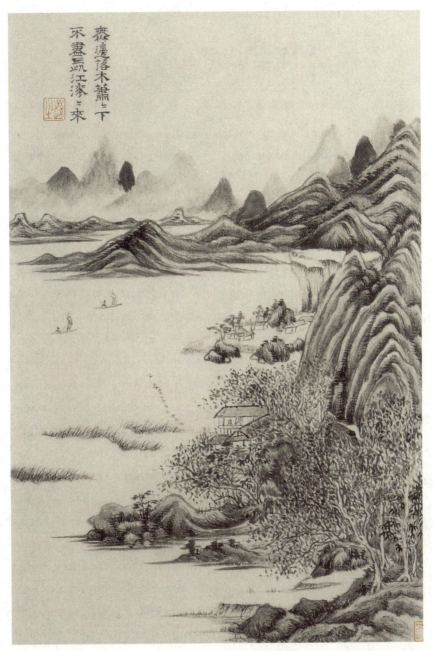

清·王时敏《杜甫诗意图》

Emperor

The emperor, or Huangdi, was the head of government and head of state in China from the beginning of the **Qin dynasty** in 221 BC until the collapse of the **Qing dynasty** (1616 – 1911). Before the Qin, the supreme Chinese leader carried the title *huang, di* or *wang*, which was equivalent to "king", and sometimes "god king".

The Emperor was referred to as "Son of Heaven", and he held absolute power over his land and people in everything. His directives and orders were considered absolutely binding, and his words sacred. Himself elevated above all his subjects, including nobles and the rest of the imperial family, he was head of the state in every respect, a leader whose words were adhered to with total obedience – at least in theory. In practice, however, different emperors from various eras ruled with more or less authority. The first emperor in China, Qin Shi Huang, one of the strongest emperors, united the country for the first time and ruled with an iron hand. One of the weakest was Guangxu, Emperor of the last dynasty, the Qing.

The title of Emperor and its affiliated responsibilities were passed down from father to son, with inheritance of the throne generally going to the first son of the Empress and Emperor. As in other societies, when male children were absent, disputes arose, and wars begun over the succession to rule. Also, as in other societies, the Empress Dowager, the mother of the Emperor, may have higher status, and may actually be the real ruler of the country, particularly under situations where the Emperor comes to the throne young. The other females have rank beginning with the Empress and continuing with the various consorts and concubines of the Emperor's harem.

皇　帝

从公元前 221 年**秦朝**建立到 1911 年
清朝 (1616 — 1911) 灭亡，这期间皇帝一
直是中国政府的首脑和国家元首。在秦朝
以前，中国最高统治者的称号为"皇"、"帝"
或"王"。

皇帝被尊称为"天子"，对其领土和
臣民有着至高无上的权力。皇帝的指示和
命令具有绝对约束力，他所说的话被称为
"圣旨"。皇帝的地位凌驾于所有臣民之上，
包括贵族和皇室其他人。他在任何方面都
是国家元首，他的话必须绝对服从——至
少在理论上如此。然而，实际上，不同

秦始皇像

时期的皇帝有着不同的威信。中国第一个
皇帝——秦始皇是最强的皇帝之一，他首
次统一全国，并用铁腕统治国家。而光绪
则是最弱的皇帝之一，他是最后一个朝
代 —— 清朝的最后一位皇帝。

皇位和皇权是世袭制，由父亲传给儿子，
一般是由皇帝和皇后的长子继承。与其他社
会一样，缺乏男性继承人会在皇宫内部引起
纷争，甚至为争夺皇位继承权而爆发战争。
皇帝的母亲——太后可能拥有更高的地位，
成为国家真正的统治者，特别是在皇帝年幼
登基的情况下。其他女性的地位则以皇后最
高，其次是皇帝的各种嫔妃、贵人。

唐·阎立本《历代帝王图》局部

Erhu

The erhu is a distinctive Chinese stringed instrument, a kind of fiddle with two strings, traditionally of silk, now mostly of metal. Played with a bow, the erhu's body, which bears the shape of a small drum, is made of red sandalwood or rosewood covered with python or snake skin on the front end. An ancestral version of the erhu dates from the **Tang dynasty** (618 – 907), and a later version was played at imperial banquets during the **Song dynasty** (960 – 1279). The erhu was a popular instrument during the **Ming** and **Qing dynasties** in the fourteenth through nineteenth centuries, when it was used in Chinese **Opera**.

Originally an ensemble instrument, the erhu has undergone a series of developments in the nineteenth and twentieth centuries that enabled it to become a solo instrument as well. The erhu performer holds the instrument upright in the manner of a cello, with the left hand cradling the instrument neck and the right hand wielding the bow. Like the violin and cello, the erhu is unfretted, a difference from the fretted **pipa**, or Chinese lute. But unlike both the western violin and cello and the Chinese pipa, the erhu is not played by pressing the string down onto the fingerboard, but rather by gliding the left hand along the length of the string while the right hand manipulates the horsehair bow between the two strings.

The erhu has a three-octave range and sounds somewhat like a violin but with a more nasal sound. It can be made to sound like the human voice, and it can imitate the song of birds. Assuming the role of the violin in western orchestras, in recent years the erhu has been made in various specifications for orchestras to create higher and lower pitched sounds as with the violin, viola, and cello.

二　胡

　　二胡是中国特有的一种弓弦乐器，有两根弦，过去为丝弦，现多为金属弦，用琴弓演奏，琴筒用紫檀木或红木蒙以蟒皮或蛇皮制成，形似小鼓。早期的二胡出现在**唐朝**（618 — 907）。**宋朝**（960 — 1279），二胡被加以改进，用于宫廷宴会上。14 至 19 世纪的**明清**时期，二胡十分流行，常用于**戏剧**伴奏。

　　二胡原是伴奏乐器，经过 19、20 世纪的一系列改进后，发展成独奏乐器。演奏者像拉大提琴一样将二胡竖起，左手持琴杆，右手操弓。与大、小提琴一样，二胡没有品，这与带品的**琵琶**不同。二胡的演奏方法与琵琶以及西方大、小提琴都不同，演奏时不是将琴弦往指板上压，而是左手在琴弦上滑动，右手来回拉动位于两根琴弦之间用马尾制成的琴弓。

　　二胡音域跨越三个八度音阶，声音略似小提琴，但鼻音感重一些。它可模仿人声和鸟鸣声。在乐队里，二胡扮演着西方乐队中小提琴的角色。近年来，人们生产出不同规格的二胡，像大、中、小提琴那样，为乐队奏出高音和低音。

二胡

公园里的小乐队演出，左数第一位是二胡演奏者

Family Relationships — Five Key Relationships

Family relationships are at the heart of Chinese culture, with the family central in Chinese cultural life. Children's duty to their parents is the root from which moral and social virtues grow. In talking to an elder person, for example, the younger person responds only after the elder has spoken. The younger individual listens with deference and should not interrupt or contradict.

The five key relationships are those between parent and child, elder brother and younger brother; husband and wife, friend and friend, and ruler and subject. Each relationship is guided by particular responsibilities according to the role played by each party. For example a parent is responsible for a child's physical care, moral guidance, and education; the corresponding responsibilities of the child involve being obedient and respectful, taking care of the parent in old age, and remembering the parent after death. Filial piety serves, moreover, as a paradigm or model for how other relationships should be conducted.

In China's traditional code of ethics, the relationship between ruler and subject patterns itself after that between parent and child. So, too, does the relationship between husband and wife, with the husband being the figure of authority (like the parent or ruler) and the wife in the subordinate role of child or subject. The elder/younger brother relationship also follows this model. The only relationship of the five key relationships that illustrates a relationship between equals is that between friends, though a hierarchy of age may obtain between friends of disparate ages. Additional relationships, such as those between employer and employee, teacher and student are bound by compelling rules of propriety. As with familial relationships, non-familial relationships are expected to endure for life.

Along with the development of society and advances in civilization, traditional code of ethics has changed. The equal relationship based on mutual respect has been established in China.

家庭关系——五种重要关系

　　家庭关系是中国文化的核心，家庭占据中国文化生活的中心位置。孝是社会道德和美德的基础。例如，与长者谈话时，晚辈必须等待长辈开口后方可回话。晚辈听长辈说话要恭敬，不得打断或反驳。

　　五种重要关系是父母和子女的关系、兄弟关系、夫妻关系、朋友关系和上下级关系。处理每种关系要根据双方所承担的特定责任。比如，父母负责子女的抚养、德育和教育；子女的相应责任包括顺从、尊重父母，父母老年时赡养他们，在父母去世后怀念他们。此外，孝也是处理其他关系的参照物和范式。

　　在中国传统的道德规范中，上下级关系是参照父母和子女的关系建立的。夫妻关系也是如此，丈夫是权威人物（类似父母或上级），妻子则像子女或下级那样处于从属地位。兄弟关系也遵循这一范式。五种关系中唯一平等的是朋友关系，不过，不同年龄的朋友之间也会产生年龄上的等级差异。此外的其他关系，如雇主和雇员、老师和学生，都受礼的制约。非家庭关系和家庭关系一样，一旦建立，人们就期待它持续终生。

　　随着社会的发展，文明的进步，传统的道德规范已经发生变化。在中国，以互相尊重为基础的平等关系得到确立。

全家福（时代图片供）

49

Fans

Fans have long been popular in China, dating from the Shang dynasty over 3 000 years ago when feathers were used to make fans. Feather fans can still be seen in China today. They are made up of a row of feathers mounted in the end of a handle.

For a long time the fans people used were mostly unfoldable round ones of silk or feathers. Paper fans came into use after the era of Sui and **Tang dynasties**, but were still in the round design. The folding fan began to be used during the **Song dynasty** and became highly popular during the **Ming** and **Qing dynasties**. The folding fans' slats were made of a hard substance such as ox bone, ivory, tortoise shell or bamboo, and were

舞蹈中也用扇子（朱　绛摄影）

covered with paper or fabric, often on which were painted elegant designs of flowers, birds, mountains, waters, etc., or calligraphy which decorated finely the cover.

Fans were useful as a way to cool oneself during spells of hot weather and were also symbolic of a person's social status. Proper manipulation of the fan, including proper forms of holding it, were considered essential for educated women. Fans are also used as props by both male and female actors in

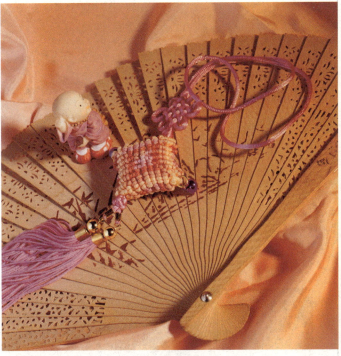

木片做的扇子

traditional Chinese classical operas, as when a young female is meeting her new love and shields her face with a fan to cover her shyness. And scholars would display their fans when thinking or writing, concealing their fans inside a sleeve or hanging it from the waist when not in use.

Fans in China today come in many shapes and sizes and are made of a myriad of materials. Their popularity as a form of visual display as well as a way to "wave wind" to cool oneself is reminiscent of ancient emperors on a trip, whose attendants followed in an honor guard behind the seated ruler, wielding long-handled large fans (called screen fans) presenting impressive manner. Both versatile and beautiful, the Chinese fan continues to be a popular item among all social classes in China and beyond.

扇　子

　　在中国，扇子长期以来一直受人喜爱。最早可以追溯到 3 000 多年前的殷商时期，就已经有羽毛做的扇子了。羽毛扇今天在中国仍能看到，扇面是一排羽毛，羽毛根部固定在扇子的把手上。

　　很长时期人们用的多是绢质团扇或羽扇，不能折叠。隋**唐**以后出现纸扇，但仍为团扇的样式。折扇出现于**宋朝**，**明清**两代变得十分流行。折扇扇骨用坚硬的物质制成，如牛骨、象牙、海龟壳或竹子，上面蒙一层纸或织物作为扇面，扇面上常绘有花鸟、山水等典雅的图案或写有书法，装饰得很精致。

　　扇子不仅是酷暑里用来降温的好工具，也是个人社会地位的象征。适当地操用扇子，包括正确的持扇方式，对于有教养的女性来说至关重要。古典戏曲里的男女演员也常用扇子作道具，年轻女子初次遇见心上人时，会用扇子遮住脸，以掩饰羞涩之情。书生在思考问题或写字时也会手摇扇子，不用时则把扇子藏在袖筒里或悬挂在腰间。

　　如今，中国的扇子有多种形状和大小，质地五花八门，

漂亮的工艺扇

人们不仅喜欢用它来"摇风"解热，还喜欢其给视觉带来的美感。这使人回想起古代皇帝出行时，他们坐在宝座上，仪仗队的侍从跟在背后，手举长柄大扇（称为障扇），威仪赫赫。中国的扇子功能众多，美观耐看，继续受到中国和国外各社会阶层人们的喜爱。

扇子常作为舞台上的道具（朱　绛摄影）

Feng Shui

Feng Shui, which combines the Chinese words for "wind" and "water", is the Chinese art of harmonizing people and their environment. It is a reflection and manifestation of Chinese philosophy in environment. Feng Shui addresses the design and layout of cities and villages, as well as houses and public buildings, for people to achieve harmony with and benefit from the environment.

Feng Shui is grounded in the idea that influences in the natural environment affect people's fortunes. In deciding where to build a temple or a home, for example, or where to situate a grave, the topography of terrain, its hills and fields and bodies of water, and their relationships to each other are analyzed. Such considerations and calculations can be quite complex; hence the need for an expert with the requisite esoteric knowledge.

Feng Shui is mysterious and even superstitious on its one side. Though not so much in use among young urban Chinese in the People's Republic, it is still used in Chinese rural areas, Hong Kong and Taiwan as well as countries like Singapore, and Malaysia, and it has practitioners, as well, in Japan and Korea. One example of a building constructed with Feng Shui in mind is the Citigroup building in Hong Kong, which was designed with a curved façade to shield it from and deflect negative elements emanating from a neighboring Bank of China building. Another example is the Cheung Kong Tower which is a "green" building inside and built with its major entrance facing east because the Feng Shui master, who advised Li Ka-shing who is the owner of the building, believed it would have a favorable effect on their wealth and fortune.

风　水

　　风水由"风"和"水"这两个字组合而成，是一门使人与环境达到和谐的中国艺术。风水是中国哲学在环境上的反映与体现。它通过调整城市、村庄以及房屋和公共建筑的设计与布局，达到人与环境和谐，并使人得益于环境。

　　人们相信自然环境影响人的命运，风水的产生就基于这一观念。例如，当选择在什么地方修建庙宇、房屋或安葬死者时，人们会分析地形、地势，考虑山川、田野以及它们彼此之间的关系。这些考虑和计算可能相当复杂，需要听取掌握必备艰深知识的专家的意见。

　　风水有神秘甚至迷信的一面，在中国城市的年轻人中已不太时兴，但在中国的农村、香港、台湾地区以及新加坡和马来西亚仍然流行，在日本和韩国也有风水师。香港的花旗大厦是根据风水建造的建筑之一，它的一面设计成弧形，以防御和抵消旁边中银大厦带来的不利因素。另一建筑是长江实业大楼。从里面看，它是一座"绿色"大厦，主入口朝向东，因为大楼主人李嘉诚聘请的风水大师相信，这种设计可以保佑他们一家的财富和好运。

香港维多利亚湾的中银大厦等建筑（时代图片供）

Festivals

Festivals in China are a popular form of celebration and entertainment for people from all walks of life. They have a long history, with the **Dragon** Boat Festival, dating from the Warring States period (475 BC – 221 BC), one of the oldest of Chinese festivals, and the celebration of the **Spring Festival**, the most important.

Besides these, other important Chinese festivals include the Qing Ming Festival, celebrated in the spring, the Moon Festival, celebrated in the fall, and the Lantern Festival, also celebrated in the spring. During the Qing Ming Festival, families pay their respects to ancestors by visiting and cleaning their tombs, and by making offerings, typically of meat, fish, fruit,

and wine, which they also share in a picnic nearby, and spirit money, which they burn in front of the tombs. The Moon Festival, known as Mid-Autumn Festival in China, takes place when the moon, theoretically, is at its fullest and brightest. As the full moon is round and the two Chinese characters *tuan* and *yuan* making up the word *tuanyuan* "reunion" also mean round, the full moon has become a symbol for family reunion. The Moon Festival brings families together to sing folk songs, display lanterns, and eat round "moon-cakes", stuffed with fruit, nuts, ham, egg-yolk, lotus-seed paste, etc.

The Lantern Festival, not surprisingly, brings people to the streets with a multitude of lanterns of great variety and color. Believed to be of Daoist origins, and dating from the **Han dynasty** (206 BC – AD 220), the Lantern Festival also includes special foods, such as *yuanxiao*, a sticky rice flour sweet stuffed dumpling, which symbolizes family unity, completeness, and happiness. As with most other Chinese festivals, the Lantern Festival is characterized by dragon dancing, playing Chinese games, and lighting and setting off firecrackers.

节日里美丽的世纪坛

节 日

　　在中国，节日是受各行各业人们所喜爱的庆祝和娱乐形式，每个节日都有悠久的历史，**端午节**的历史可追溯到战国时期（前 475 — 前 221），是中国最古老的节日之一，**春节**则是最重要的节日。

　　此外，其他重要的中国节日包括春天的清明节和秋天的中秋节，还有也是在春天的元宵节（灯节）。清明节的时候，家庭成员通过扫墓和祭奠来缅怀祖先，祭品通常是肉、鱼、水果、酒和纸钱。祭奠用的食品，他们会在附近与亡灵分享，所祭的纸钱，会在墓前烧掉。中秋节是理论上月亮在一年里最圆最亮的那一天。由于"团圆"这两个字的意思都是"圆"，美满、圆圆的月亮就成为家庭团聚的象征。中秋节的时候，一家人会聚在一起唱民歌、点灯笼、吃圆形的月饼。月饼里有水果、果仁、火腿、蛋黄、莲蓉等做的馅。

舞龙（毛尧泉摄影）

　　元宵节又名灯节。在这个节日，人们会打着灯笼，来到挂满各式各样、色彩缤纷的灯笼的大街上赏灯。据说元宵节起源于道家，历史可追溯到**汉朝**（前206 — 220）。元宵节也有特殊的食品，如糯米做的有甜馅的元宵，象征家庭团结、和睦与幸福。和其他大多数中国节日一样，元宵节典型的庆祝活动包括舞龙、中国传统游戏和燃放烟花爆竹。

端午节赛龙舟（时代图片供）

Forbidden City

The Forbidden City, which is today's Palace Museum, is located in the center of the ancient city of Beijing. Better known as *Gugong* "former palace" in China, it served as the imperial palace during the **Ming** and **Qing dynasties** which ruled China from the late fourteenth century to the early twentieth century successively. Located directly north of Tiananmen Square, and accessible through Tiananmen Gate, the Forbidden City is comprised of 980 buildings with 8 704 rooms.

Construction of the Forbidden City began in the early fifteenth century and took some 200 000 men fourteen years. In 1911, with the abdication of the last Chinese Qing **emperor**, Pu Yi, the Forbidden City, after serving as home to 24 Ming and Qing emperors, lost its role as China's political center, though the last emperor remained in the Forbidden City until 1924.

As the Chinese word *huang* "yellow" has the same sound as the first syllable of *huangdi* "emperor", and in theories of **Yin** and **Yang** and the Five Elements, yellow matches earth that occupies the central position as the central orthodox color. It became the symbol and color of the royal family, dominating in the Forbidden City. Roofs are constructed with yellow glazed tiles, many palace decorations are yellow, and yellow bricks line many passageways. Other colors, however, also appear, with vibrant red columns, blue and green painted dragons and phoenixes, and considerable gold decoration.

The Forbidden City is layed out in a gridded square, with interlocking gates and courtyards, the most important in the inner part. It was divided into an Inner Court and an Outer Court. The Inner Court housed the

Emperor and his family and their entourage, and provided halls and rooms for the conduct of day-to-day government business. The Outer Court provided halls for court meetings and ceremonial occasions, and housed the Department of the Palace, the Imperial Library, the Imperial Archives, the Imperial Stables and so on. The Crown Prince's residence was also in the Outer Court.

故宫角楼

紫　禁　城

　　紫禁城即今天的故宫博物院（简称故宫），坐落于北京古城的中央。
紫禁城是**明朝**和**清朝**的皇宫。这两个朝代从 14 世纪下半叶到 20 世纪初
先后统治中国。紫禁城位于天安门广场的正北方，可由天安门进入，由
980 座建筑组成，有房屋 8 704 间。

　　紫禁城始建于公元 15 世纪早期，由约二十万人用 14 年时间建成。
随着 1911 年清朝末代**皇帝**溥仪的逊位，紫禁城这座住过 24 位明清皇帝

紫禁城全貌

的皇宫失去了中国政治中心的地位，不过，溥仪在宫中一直住到 1924 年。

　　由于"黄"与"皇"同音，也由于在**阴阳**五行学说中"黄"与"土"相配，土居中，所以黄色为中央正色，成为皇族的色彩和象征。黄色是紫禁城的主色调，屋顶铺的是黄琉璃瓦，宫中很多饰品是黄色的，众多通道铺着黄砖。当然，其他颜色也有，如大红柱子、蓝绿两色绘制的龙和凤以及大量金色饰品。

　　紫禁城的布局为网格状的矩形，门庭交错，中心部分最为重要。紫禁城分外朝与内廷，内廷是皇帝、皇室人员及随从居住的地方，也有供皇帝处理日常政务的殿堂和房间；外朝有用于皇帝举行朝会和典礼的大殿、处理皇宫事务的内务府、皇家图书馆文渊阁、档案馆内阁大库、皇家马厩上驷院等，太子居住的南三所也在外朝。

Gate of Heavenly Peace

The Gate of Heavenly Peace, *Tiananmen*, was the main entryway to the Imperial Palace. In the beginning it was not called the Gate of Heavenly Peace and was twice built and destroyed by fire. In 1651 under the **Qing Emperor** Shunzhi, the gate tower was rebuilt in the original style and renamed Tiananmen, or "Gate of Heavenly Peace".

A monumental structure, the base of the gate is more than thirty-six feet high. Set on a foundation of white marble, the base is built of large bricks and contains five arched gateways in the city wall. Standing above the base is the massive gate tower, constructed in palace style, with its roof more than a hundred feet from the ground. Its roof is covered with the same type of yellow-glazed tiles that cover the roofs of all the Imperial buildings. The roof has world-famous carvings of various animals, including ten dragon heads, whose function is to protect the palace and its inhabitants from harm.

In front of the gate are two stone lions, a female playing with a cub, and a male with his hand on a large ball. Among the explanations of their significance is that the Emperor was so powerful that the king of beasts was reduced to the role of playful watcher at the gate. Also part of the structure are four large white columns, two in front of the gate facing south and two behind it facing north, each with another animal (*hou*) on top. They were set up there presumably to keep watch for the emperor and to admonish him if he remained inside or outside the palace walls for too long. Today, the Gate remains a central focus, with the central part covered by a giant portrait of the Communist leader Mao Zedong (1893 – 1976).

天 安 门

天安门是进入紫禁城的正门。一开始它不叫天安门，建了两次，又两次毁于大火。1651 年，**清朝**顺治**皇帝**命人按原式样重建城楼，改名为天安门。

天安门是一座不朽的建筑。城台高 36 英尺多，由大长方砖建成，矗立在汉白玉基座上。城墙上有五座拱门。城台上坐落着宫廷风格、气势雄伟的城楼，楼顶距地面一百多英尺，上面覆盖着与紫禁城所有建筑房顶相同的黄琉璃瓦，并有闻名于世的各种动物造型。这些动物，其中包括 10 个龙头，起着庇护宫殿及其居住者的作用。

城门前雄踞着两座石狮，一座是雌狮戏子，另一座是雄狮踏球。石狮造型亦有诸多说法，其中一种是：在强大的皇帝面前，百兽之王也沦为嬉戏的城门看守。城楼前和城楼后还各有两座称为华表的高大白色立柱，顶上各蹲着一头异兽（犼）。它们均面朝南北，起着为皇帝值守的作用，如果皇帝在宫里或宫外停留过久，它们会发出吼叫声提醒皇帝。今天，天安门仍是万众瞩目的焦点。在城楼的中心位置，挂有一幅共产党领袖毛泽东（1893 — 1976）的巨型肖像。

天安门

Giant Panda

The Giant Panda is beloved by the people of China and other countries. A national treasure in China, the giant panda is protected by law. Recent genetic tests have confirmed that pandas are related to bears, with which they have more than a little in common, including their size, shape, and ways of walking and climbing.

The panda has an ancient heritage, believed to have come into existence two to three million years ago. Early pandas were carnivores, but over time, they evolved to consume a diet mostly of **bamboo** and, occasionally, meat.

Immediately recognizable because of its white coat on more than half of the body and distinctive black marks on the ears, around the eyes, and elsewhere on its body, the giant panda has become an informal national icon for China, with its image now found on many Chinese commemorative coins. The panda inhabits mountainous regions in Sichuan and Shaanxi, and because of an extremely low reproductive rate, it is an endangered species.

Giant pandas express themselves by making a variety of sounds that include bleating, honking, barking, and growling, though they don't make the customary roar of black and brown bears. It is five times more expensive to take care of a panda in a zoo than it is to care for the next most expensive animal, the elephant. And thus, there are only a handful of zoos worldwide that have pandas as part of their population, including, of course, the Beijing Zoo.

The panda remains a highly visible emblem, with logos that include images of pandas used by restaurants, such as Panda Garden and Panda Palace, as well as the fast food chain, Panda Express.

大　熊　猫

大熊猫受到中国人民和世界各地人们的喜爱。作为中国的国宝，大熊猫受法律保护。近期的基因测试表明，熊猫和熊是近亲，而且它们在个头、外型以及行走和攀爬方式上都有很多相似之处。

熊猫是一种古老的物种，据信已经存在了二三百万年。熊猫最初是食肉动物，但随着时间的推移，已经慢慢演变成杂食动物，以**竹**为主食，偶尔也吃肉。

大熊猫长相独特，全身多半为白色，双耳、眼周和身体其他一些部位为黑色。大熊猫已经成为中国的非正式象征，许多纪念币上都有熊猫的图像。熊猫栖息在四川、陕西等地的山区，繁殖率极低，属于濒危物种。

大熊猫通常不像黑熊和棕熊那样吼叫，而是发出咩咩、昂昂、吠叫、咆哮等各种声音来表达自己的情绪。在动物园里，照料一只大熊猫的花费是照料第二昂贵的动物大象的五倍。因此，全球仅有几所动物园拥有大熊猫，当然北京动物园是其中之一。

熊猫图案随处可见，出现在很多徽标上，包括以熊猫为形象标志的餐馆，如熊猫花园、熊猫宫以及熊猫快餐等。

熊猫（朱　绛摄影）

Great Wall

The Great Wall of China began to be constructed in the Spring and Autumn period and the Warring States Period during the seventh century BC when walls were built as defensive fortifications along their boards by different kingdoms to protect themselves. The first **Emperor** Qin Shihuang, who wanted to protect his country from invaders of the north, after unifying the country, joined together these walls. Most of the Great Wall of today was built during the last eighty years of the **Ming dynasty**, from about 1560 to 1640.

长城雪景

The wall is built of varied materials, depending on what was available locally. Badaling Great Wall of Beijing, for instance, was constructed mainly from boulder strips and gray bricks, whereas before the Ming Dynasty, on flat grounds great walls were made of rammed loess. In western desert portions where there is a lack of bricks and stones, read, branches of Chinese tamarisk and gravels were even used.

One of the "Seven Ancient Wonders of the World", the Great Wall was made a UNESCO World Heritage Site in 1987, and it remains a premier tourist attraction, and a source of great pride to the Chinese. Among the many myths and claims about the Great Wall is the claim that it is the only man-made object on earth that is visible to the naked eye on a spaceship. Whether or not it is visible from astrospace, the Great Wall is a monumental achievement, spanning centuries, involving hundreds of

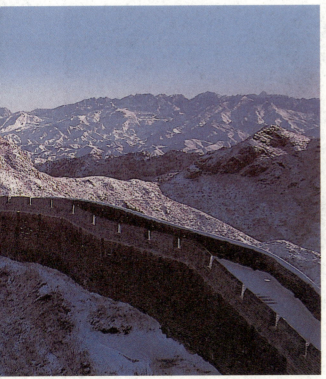

thousands of workers. Its nearly 4 000 miles extending through nine provinces and regions continue to inspire amazement and awe – and shortness of breath – among the many who have the opportunity to climb even a small part of it.

长 城

　　长城从公元前7世纪的春秋战国时期就开始修建了。当时，各个诸侯国为保护自己的安全，曾在边界筑墙作为防御工事，秦始皇统一中国后，为阻挡北方游牧民族的入侵，将这些墙垣连接成为一个整体。现存长城大部分建于**明朝**后期的八十余年间（约 1560 — 1640）。

　　修筑长城时，人们就地取材，使用了多种材料。例如，北京附近的八达岭明长城使用的材料主要是条石和青砖。明代以前在平地上修建的长城则用黄土夯筑，在西部砖石缺少的沙漠地区，人们甚至用芦苇、红柳枝条和砂砾修筑长城。

金山岭长城

　　长城是"世界古代七大奇迹"之一，1987 年被联合国教科文组织列为世界文化遗产，是中国的首要旅游点，也是中国人的骄傲。关于长城，有很多神话和夸张的传闻，其中一种说法就是，长城是从太空船上唯一能用肉眼看到的地球上的建筑物。不管能否从宇宙空间看到，长城都是一项丰碑式的成就。它跨越许多世纪，耗费几十万人力，绵延近四千英里，穿过九个省区，让所有有幸攀登哪怕是一小段长城的人们都不禁叹为观止、难以置信。

金山岭长城（孙述学摄影）

Guanxi

*G*uanxi refers exclusively to the Chinese form of networking, using connections to get things done. For the Chinese, knowing who is as important as knowing how. And certainly knowing how to get to the right "who" in the complex network of relationships constitutes a form of *guanxi*, as does knowing how to subtly exert the requisite pressure on "whom", which is another facet of it. *Guanxi* is almost necessary in finding a job, a place to live, a school for one's children, even a marriage partner. *Guanxi* is important for Chinese people and is equally helpful in a larger sphere, such as in overseas business contacts.

Based on the principle of moral obligation, returning favors done, *guanxi* is rooted in kinship relationships, in family ties that require reciprocity and taking care of one another. However, it is not normally used to describe relationships within a family, as it is not typically used to describe conventional social relationships such as that of employer and employee.

Non-relatives and foreigners can also become part of the *guanxi* equation through marriage or through friendships. Other ties that build *guanxi* are mutual experiences such as school ties, shared military experience, or working for a particular company or in a similar field.

In the broadest sense, *guanxi* stands for any kind of relationship. In practice, these tend more often than not to be business related, and exist on both the individual and the company level. And though the English words "connections" and "relationships" capture something of the meaning of *guanxi*, they don't capture its full significance or its cultural importance.

关　系

　　关系特指具有中国特色的人际关系网，指利用人际关系办事情。对于中国人来说，认识什么人和知道怎么办同等重要。懂得如何在复杂的人际关系网中找到合适的人，显然是关系的一面；而懂得如何微妙地对其施加所必需的影响，则是关系的另一面。找工作，找地方住，为孩子找学校，甚至找对象，都要有关系。对于中国人来说，关系十分重要，在更大的范围内，例如在国际商业联系中，关系同样有帮助。

　　基于道德义务和礼尚往来的原则，关系植根于亲属关系、家庭纽带，要求亲属和家庭成员互惠互利，互相照顾。但是"关系"这个词通常不用来指家庭内部的关系，也一般不用来指常规的社会关系，如雇主和雇员之间的关系。

　　非亲属以及外国人通过婚姻或友谊也可建立关系。其他建立关系的纽带包括共同经历，如校友、战友或同事、同行。

　　广义上说，"关系"可以指任何一种联系。实际上，关系多半与商业有关，在个人和公司层面上都存在。尽管英语词 *connections*（联系）和 *relationship*（关系）都有"关系"的部分意思，但却都未能抓住这个词的全部含义及其文化上的重要性。

朋友关系很重要

Han Dynasty

The Han dynasty (206 BC – AD 220) followed immediately after the **Qin dynasty** (221 BC – 206 BC). Lasting for more than four centuries, the Han dynasty is considered one of the greatest and most important in Chinese history. In fact, even today, people of the Chinese ethnic majority refer to themselves as the Han people.

The Han dynasty includes two dynasties: the Earlier Han and the Later Han. The Western and earlier dynasty (206 BC – AD 9) was established by a rebel leader named Liu Bang with Chang'an (today Xi'an) as its capital, and the Eastern and later Han dynasty (25 – 220) was reestablished by Liu Xiu, the nineth generation decendent of Liu Bang with Luoyang (today Luoyang of Henan) as its capital, each lasting around two centuries. During the Western Han and the Eastern Han, agriculture and commerce flourished, and the population multiplied. China's cultural reach increased dramatically, extending to the Korean Peninsula, Central Asia and Vietnam.

During the Han dynasty, China officially became a **Confucian** country, as the **Emperor**, Wu, dismissed **Daoism** as not suitable for China. Establishing Confucianism (though combined with some Legalist modifications) as the state doctrine prepared the way for an extensive civil service system that included many days of compulsory examinations focusing on classic Confucian texts, such as the *Analects*, for those wishing to serve in the Confucian bureaucracy.

The Han dynasty can be compared in many respects to the Roman Empire, which was roughly contemporaneous with it. Both the Han and the Romans were superpowers, notable for their strong militaries. Both extracted tribute from conquered regions. And both established important trade routes, the Han, what would become known as the "Silk Road" for the export of its most important commodity.

汉　朝

汉光武帝刘秀

汉朝（前 206 — 220）紧随**秦朝**（前 221 — 前 206）之后。汉朝的统治延续了四个多世纪，被视为中国历史上最伟大、最重要的一个朝代。时至今日，占中国人口多数的民族仍叫汉族，他们称自己为汉人。

汉朝包括前汉和后汉两个时期。前汉史称西汉（前 206 — 9），是一位名叫刘邦的起义领袖建立的，都城在长安（今陕西西安）；后汉史称东汉（25 — 220），是刘邦的九世孙刘秀重建的，都城在洛阳（今河南洛阳）。这两个朝代各延续了大约两个世纪。在西汉和东汉时期，农业和商业都蓬勃发展，人口成倍增加。中国文化的影响力急剧增强，传播到朝鲜半岛、中亚和越南。

在汉朝，**儒家**学说开始正式为统治者所采纳。汉武帝认为**道家**学说不适合中国，将之废黜，改尊儒术，在此基础上建立了一个广泛文官制度。要想成为这一儒家官僚体系中的一员，就必须通过为期多天的考试，考试内容主要围绕儒家经典，如《**论语**》。

在许多方面，汉朝和罗马帝国都有相似之处，二者大约存在于同一时期，都是以强大的军事实力闻名的超级大国，都迫使所征服地区纳贡，都建立了重要的商路。后来的"丝绸之路"就是从汉朝开始出现的，以便出口其最重要的商品。

东汉时期的丝织品

Hanban

Hanban is the shorthand name for China's "Office of Chinese Language Council International" (OCLCI). Established in 1987, it was originally named "National Office for Teaching Chinese as a Foreign Language" (NOTCFL). Its goal is to enhance the understanding of Chinese language and culture around the world, mainly but not exclusively through its "Confucius Institutes", located in many countries, with the central institute office in Beijing. The Chinese government considers the promotion of Chinese language and culture worldwide of paramount importance and has decreed that the leading group of the Hanban be composed of the leaders of eleven departments of the State Council.

Among the many aspects of the work of Hanban's Confucius Institutes is organizing training for teachers of Chinese as a Foreign Language at the elementary, high school, and university levels. It develops teaching materials, designs curriculums, and organizes conferences on the teaching of Chinese as a Foreign Language. It sponsors programs and coordinates for schools, corporations, and other agencies abroad, such as foreign ministries of education, school districts, and state governmental agencies.

One of its biggest current projects is with the College Board in the United States, in which US teachers of Chinese are brought to China for intensive seminars on teaching Chinese as a Foreign Language; Chinese volunteer teachers are sent to the US to work in local schools, paired with American teachers; educational administrators from China visit the US, while those from the US visit China to better understand each system's educational policies and practices; curriculum resources are jointly developed; and teacher certification is cooperatively sponsored and administered.

The Hanban office remains an important mechanism for the spread of Chinese language and culture throughout the world. It offers opportunities for cross cultural exchanges and the promotion of intercultural understanding.

汉　办

　　汉办是中国"国家汉语国际推广领导小组办公室"的简称。汉办成立于 1987 年，一开始名叫"国家对外汉语教学领导小组办公室"。其宗旨是通过其资助的孔子学院等机构，增进世界各国对汉语和中国文化的了解。现在许多国家都设有孔子学院，学院的总部设在北京。中国政府认为，在全世界推广汉语和中华文化具有头等重要的意义，并决定汉办领导小组由国务院 11 个部门的领导组成。

　　汉办下属的孔子学院的众多工作包括培训大、中、小学的对外汉语教师等。汉办负责开发教材，制定课程大纲，组织对外汉语教学会议，并赞助和协调国外学校、社会团体以及外国教育部、校区和州政府机构之类其他外国机构所举办的项目。

　　汉办目前最大的项目之一是与美国大学理事会的合作项目。该项目将美国的中文教师送到中国进行对外汉语教学的集中研修；将中国的志愿教师送往美国地方院校与美国教师结对教学；中美教育管理者到对方国家考察，以加深对彼此教育制度、教育政策和实践的了解；中美双方共同开发课程资源，合作资助和实施教师资格认证。

　　汉办是中国向世界传播汉语和中国文化的重要机构。同时，它也为加强跨文化交流、加深不同文化间的了解创造了机会。

汉办办公大楼

I Ching
(Book of Changes)

The *I Ching,* an important ancient classic in Chinese culture, is a collection of observations that the Chinese have used for centuries as a repository of wisdom and as a basis for making predictions. Many people use the *I Ching* as a guide to living and decision making, envisioning it as a kind of oracle for the future. Carl Jung, the famous western psychologist, once remarked that the *I Ching* offers neither proof nor results, but rather, that as part of nature, it waits to be discovered.

Central to the philosophy embedded in the *I Ching* are concepts that include a balancing of opposite forces in dynamic equilibrium, an understanding of the unfolding nature of events in an evolving fashion, and accepting change as an inescapable fact of life. The symbolism of the *I Ching* is contained in a set of hexagrams, or abstract arrangements of lines. Some lines are solid, while others are broken, with the solid lines representing **Yang**, or the creative principle and the broken lines representing **Yin**, or the receptive principle. The hexagrams are divided into trigrams, or sets of three lines each. Each of the sixty-four hexagrams contains six horizontal lines on top of one another.

As shows in the drawings:

The *I Ching* is believed to be at the center of Chinese philosophical thought with links to both **Daoism** and **Confucianism**. One of the five Confucian Classics, of which another is the **Book of Songs**, important commentaries have been written on the *I Ching* by Confucian and Neo-Confucian scholars.

Among the flags of Asian nations, that of the former Republic of Vietnam (South Vietnam) contained the trigram made up of three solid lines, representing Heaven (also South). The flag of South Korea includes four of the trigrams representing Heaven, Earth, Water, and Fire as they surround the YinYang symbol.

伏羲八卦

《易 经》

　　《易经》是中国文化的重要典籍，它是描述事物变化规律的一个系统，中国人几千年来一直将它视为智慧的宝藏和预测未来之事的基础。许多人使用《易经》作为自己生活和决策的指南，把它看作一种预知未来的卜辞。著名西方心理学家卡尔·荣格（Carl Jung）曾说，《易经》既不提供证明，也不提供结果，而是作为自然的一部分，在等待被发现。

　　《易经》所内含的中心哲学思想包括：平衡对立力量使之处于动态均衡状态，把事件理解为一个不断演化、发展的过程，把变化作为无法避免的生活事实接受下来。《易经》的象征性包含在被称为八卦的一套符号中，这些符号由代表阳的 — 和代表阴的 −− 组成，每三个 — 或 −− 组合在一起，共有八个组合方式，称为八卦，如图所示：

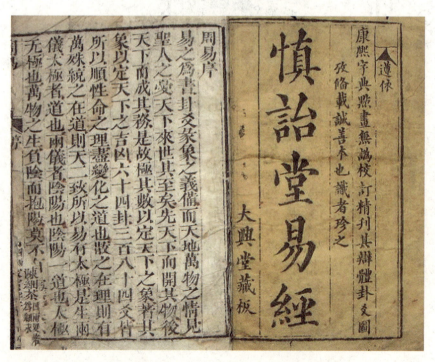

《易经》书影

　　两个卦合在一起，可形成一个由六道阴线或阳线组成的复合符号，这种复合符号共有 64 个，称为 64 卦。

　　《易经》据信是中国哲学思想的核心成分，与**道家**和**儒家**都有关系。《易经》是包括《**诗经**》在内的儒家五部经典之一，孔子和新儒学的学者都对《易经》作出了重要解释和评论。

　　在亚洲国家中，过去越南的国旗上曾有一个由三条直线组成的八卦符——乾，代表天（以及南方）。韩国国旗上有四个八卦符围绕阴阳图，分别代表天、地、水、火。

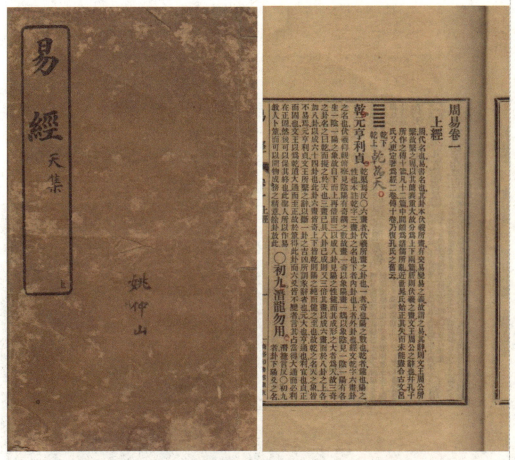

商务印书馆藏版《易经》

Inventions

The Chinese claim a number of important inventions, among them, the abacus, the compass, gunpowder, fireworks, kites, paper, the rudder, and **silk**, among others.

The world's first compass, called *sinan* "south-indicator" dating from the Warring States period (475BC – 221BC), was made in the form of a magnetic spoon placed in the center of a square bronze plate representing the earth. By the time of the **Song dynasty** (960 – 1279), the spoon was replaced by a needle like it is today. For a long time this new compass was used by **Feng Shui** masters to determine the proper direction a house or a grave should face. It wasn't until the eleventh century that it was widely used for navigation.

节日天安门广场燃放的烟花

Paper was invented during the **Han dynasty** (206 BC – AD 220). Bark and hemp were used in one form of paper, silk cloth in others. Both crude and fine papers were produced. Ink, too, was invented during the Han dynasty, though it wasn't until the **Tang dynasty** (618 – 907) that woodblock printing was invented. In Song Dynasty a Chinese printer by the name of Bi Sheng invented movable type, hundreds of years ahead of the first Gutenberg bibles printed in Germany during the fifteenth century.

明代的墨

Perhaps the most famous of Chinese inventions is gunpowder, also invented during the Tang dynasty. Chinese scientists discovered the explosive properties of a mixture of sulfur, charcoal, and potassium nitrate, with both entertainment and military value. Firecrackers have long been part of Chinese (and other countries') holiday celebrations; rockets for military and festive use were launched from bamboo tubes.

In the last few hundred years, inventions, especially new technologies have shifted to the west. But with large recent investments in education, science, and technology, China can be expected to return as a place where inventions are once again made.

发 明

　　中国拥有一系列重要的发明，如算盘、指南针、火药、烟花、风筝、纸、舵和**丝绸**。

　　世界上最早的指南仪是战国时期（前 475 — 前 221）发明的司南，由一个代表大地的方形铜盘和盘子中央的一个磁勺组成。到了**宋朝**（960 — 1279），磁勺被磁针取代，这种新的指南仪称为指南针、罗盘针或罗盘。很长时间，罗盘被风水师用来确定房址和坟址的朝向，直到 11 世纪才被用于航海。

　　纸是**汉朝**（前 206 — 220）发明的，分为两种：一种以树皮和麻作原料，另一种以丝织品作原料，粗纸和精纸都生产。墨也发明于汉代，不过直到**唐朝**（618 — 907）才发明雕版印刷术。宋代，一位名叫毕升的印刷工

万安罗盘（徽州文化博物馆供）

首创活字印刷。比 15 世纪中期德国的第一本谷登堡 (Gutenberg) 圣经早了数百年。

　　火药也许是中国最著名的发明，也出现于唐朝。中国古代科学家发现硫磺、木炭和硝混合在一起具有爆炸性，可用于娱乐和军事目的。燃放烟花一直是中国（和其他国家）节日庆典的节目；用于军事和节日庆祝的火箭可用竹筒发射。

　　最近几百年里，发明，特别是新技术的研发，转移到了西方。但是随着中国近年来在教育、科学和技术上的巨大投资，中国有望再度成为发明创造之乡。

汉代司南

Jade

Jade culture has had a four-thousand-year history in China. Associated with nobility, dignity, and social status, and known as a symbol of virtue, jade possesses an exalted position among valuable materials, assuming an importance that transcends that of silver and gold. A Chinese proverb notes that "there is a price for gold but no price for jade". In the Warring States period, a large top-quality jade ring "Heshibi" was considered "worth a string of towns". Other proverbs about jade refer less to its monetary value than its moral and spiritual significance, as the proverb that "unpolished jade never shines", which suggests that one must be educated to become useful. Jade, in fact, is associated with a number of enviable qualities and attributes, including beauty, blessings, eternity, holiness, love, loyalty, and longevity.

商代玉器

Among the uses of jade are its decorative function, as jewelry, and its use in worship and burial rites. Jade articles have been found in tombs before the **Qin Dynasty** (221 BC – 206 BC). But jade was put to other uses as well. The famous Yuan dynasty (1206 – 1368) **emperor** Kublai

商店里琳琅满目的玉雕摆件

Khan had an enormous jade vessel with the size of a bathtub made, which he filled with wine on festive occasions to entertain guests. Engraved with horses and dragons, it is the largest jade object in China. Another large jade object, made during the reign of Emperor Qianlong (1736 – 1795), is a monumental sculpture depicting the ancient hero, the Great Yu, taming a flood with the working people, which took years to carve, after the monumental jade stone was transported more than 4 000 miles to Beijing.

Today, jade objects are produced in all major cities in China, in workshops and in factories. Popular with people from all walks of life, rich and poor, jade objects, which are believed to possess soul, bring contentment and consolation to their owners.

玉

　　玉文化在中国已有四千年的历史。由于与高贵、尊严和社会地位联系在一起，又是美德的象征，因此玉在各种珍贵材料中拥有崇高地位，被赋予超越金银的重要内涵。中国有句俗语叫做"黄金有价玉无价"。战国时期，有一件上好品质的玉璧"和氏璧"曾被视为"价值连城"。另外一些俗语注重的不是玉的金钱价值，而是其道德和精神意义，如"玉不琢，不成器"，告诉人们要接受教育，才能做有用之材。事实上，玉总是与一些令人羡慕的品性联系在一起，如美丽、祝福、不朽、神圣、爱情、忠诚和长寿。

　　玉具有装饰作用，可被制成首饰，也常用于祭祀和葬礼仪式中。早在**秦朝**（前221 — 前206）以前陪葬品里就有玉器。玉还有其他用途。元朝（1206 — 1368）著名的皇帝忽必烈命人为他做了一个浴缸大小的巨大玉质容器，节日庆典时，里面注满酒，招待宾客。容器上刻有马和

现代玉雕摆件

清代白玉雕刻的笔架

龙的图案，是中国最大的玉器。另一件大型玉器于清乾隆年间（1736 —
1795）制成。这是一座纪念雕像，刻画了大禹这位古代英雄和劳动人民
治理洪水的情景。玉料从四千多英里之外运到北京，费时数年才雕刻完成。

现在，中国的大部分城市里都有玉器作坊和工厂。各行各业的人们，
不论贫富，都很喜欢玉器。他们认为玉石具有灵性，可以给主人带来满
足和慰藉。

新石器时代的玉龙

Journey to the West

Journey to the West is among the most famous and important of Chinese literary works. A classic work of Chinese fiction written in the **Ming dynasty** (1368 – 1644), this novel of one hundred chapters is generally attributed to the scholar Wu Cheng'en. Considered one of the four great Classical Novels of Chinese literature, *Journey to the West* is also known by other titles in the west, including *Monkey* translated by Arthur Waley, after the protagonist, the monkey king.

The novel is a picaresque novel that describes the adventures of a **Tang dynasty** Buddhist monk on a pilgrimage to India to acquire sacred Buddhist scriptures, Sutras, which he is supposed to bring to the Chinese capital of Chang'an (today Xi'an). On his way, the monk, Xuan Zang, accepts three supernatural beings as his followers – Monkey (the monkey king), Pig (pig-monster), and Friar Sand (river-monster) as well as a dragon prince in disguise as a white horse, and runs into various dangerous situations. Under the protection of his disciples and with the help of gods and the Buddha, he manages to get out of danger each time. The novel is at one and the same time an adventure story, a work of spiritual insight, and an allegory of the individual self searching for enlightenment.

In the manner of Tolkien's *Lord of the Rings*, the four undergo dangerous challenges and threatening attacks, fighting off demons, spider women, and other assorted monsters. It takes 14 years, but the journey is ultimately successfully completed. Based on an actual journey by a Tang dynasty monk of the same name, *Journey to the West* is the best known but not the only fictionalized account of the real journey. Some earlier accounts, in fact, are believed to derive from and overlap with the monkey god from the popular Hindu epic, the *Ramayana*.

《西　游　记》

　　《西游记》是中国最著名、最重要的文学作品之一。这部中国古典小说有 100 回，创作于**明朝**（1368 —— 1644），作者是吴承恩。《西游记》是中国四大古典名著之一，其英文本除了 *Journey to the West* 外，还有亚瑟·韦利（Arthur Waley）翻译的 *Monkey*，书名取自书中的主人公孙悟空。

　　这部历险传奇小说讲述**唐朝**一个名叫玄奘的和尚前往印度求取佛经，并将佛经带回首都长安（即今天的陕西西安）的历险故事。取经途中，玄奘收了三个徒弟，即孙悟空（猴王）、猪八戒（猪妖）、沙僧（河妖）和龙太子化身的一匹白马，经历了许多劫难，但在徒弟的保护和众多天神的帮助下，每一次都转危为安。这部小说既是一个历险故事，又是一部精神领悟作品和一则个人寻求自身启蒙的寓言。

　　《西游记》和托尔金的《指环王》有些相似。四人经历各种危险挑战和威胁性袭击，打退妖魔、蜘蛛精等各种妖怪，来回行程共花了 14 年时间，最终成功取回真经。小说取材自唐朝和尚玄奘的真实经历，是描写这段经历的诸多小说里最著名的一部。事实上，有人认为之前关于这段经历的一些描述取材自印度通俗史诗《罗摩衍那》中神猴的形象。

唐玄奘

Kites

K ites have long been valued in China for their artistic value, for entertainment and amusement, and for their military use. China is generally believed to be the birthplace of Kites. The earliest record in relation to kites says that Lu Ban (507 BC – 444 BC), who is worshipped as the ancestor of carpenters in China, made a wooden bird for the purpose of spying on the enemy. In the confrontation between Chu and Han, Liu Bang's top general Han Xin used kites with whistles to confuse enemy soldiers in order to defeat them. Kites were also used in ancient times to measure the distance between two places, to send out rescue messages, and even for people to glide with from a high place.

The kite has been considered as a forerunner of airplanes. The National Aeronautics and Space Museum in Washington DC, in the US, includes Chinese kites among its numerous airplanes, describing them as the earliest aircraft. Kites have also been used to conduct scientific experiments, as exemplified by the American scientist and diplomat Benjamin Franklin's studies of lightning and his invention of the lightning rod, with the aid of a kite. And kites have been used in the sea as well as the sky, as fishermen on a Pacific island troll with them.

During the **Tang dynasty** (618 – 907), a period of great cultural accomplishment, kites became a popular amusement and were fitted with **bamboo** flutes that would be blown by winds in the air, creating a ringing sound, which added to the pleasure of kite flying. In later periods, kites were also flown after dark, with lanterns attached, making an appealing visual display of lights against the night sky. Because flying a kite requires being out of doors in good weather (spring is a popular time for kites), kite flying today is considered good for one's health, a bonus added to its manifold pleasures.

风　筝

　　在中国，风筝因其艺术、娱乐价值和军事用途而一直受到重视。中国被公认为风筝发明地。与风筝相关的最早记录是，被中国木匠尊奉为祖师爷的鲁班（约前 507 — 前 444）做了一只木鸟，用来侦察敌情。楚汉相争时，刘邦的大将韩信曾用带哨子的风筝迷惑敌人，然后将其击败。风筝还曾被用来测量两地之间的距离，送求救信，甚至供人从高处往下滑翔。

　　风筝被视为飞机的鼻祖。美国华盛顿的国家航空航天博物馆把中国风筝同数不清的飞机陈列在一起，认为风筝就是最早的飞行器。风筝还用于科学试验。美国科学家和外交家本杰明·富兰克林在研究闪电和发明避雷针时就利用了风筝。风筝不仅用于空中，还用于海洋，在太平洋的一个岛屿上，渔民用它钓鱼。

　　在文化鼎盛时期的**唐朝**，风筝是一项受欢迎的娱乐活动。那时，人们给风筝安上了**竹**笛，竹笛在空中被风吹动，发出悦耳的声音，更增加了放风筝的乐趣。后来，人们也在晚上放风筝。他们给风筝挂上灯笼，让风筝在夜幕的衬托下，发出赏心悦目的光。由于放风筝需要在户外晴朗的日子进行（春天是放风筝的最好季节），如今放风筝被当作一项有益健康的活动，这是有趣的风筝带来的又一大好处。

各种各样的风筝

Kung Fu

In the west kung fu is known as a form of Chinese martial art. In China the word for martial art is *wushu* whereas kung fu mainly refers to an individual's attainment or proficiency in terms of martial art. Like all forms of martial art, kung fu (wushu) combines self defense and exercise, combat techniques and sport, art and discipline, philosophy and way of life.

As with many aspects of Chinese culture, the origin of the martial arts dates back to ancient times, with historical record showing that early forms of martial art existed as early as in the Shang dynasty (1600 BC – 1046 BC). By around AD 500, Buddhist monks at the Shaolin Monastery in central China had developed a form of martial art to exercise their bodies and protect themselves against attacks by bandits. And it was directly from this Shaolin fighting style that many of modern martial arts techniques have developed, of which there are currently more than 1 000 styles and forms.

Daoism, with its emphasis on the importance of *Qi* and exercise of *Qigong*, has played no less a role in the development of kung fu (wushu), as the latter requires of the practitioner a strict code of physical and mental discipline that has its basis in Daoism, following the true Dao, or way. To attain proficiency in the dual aspects of mental and physical discipline takes a high degree of devotion and dedication. Quite a number of kung fu styles derive from movements of animals, with various blocks, attacks, and stances derived from and done in imitation of particular animals' movements. A tiger style, for example might be used to break a rock, a standard martial arts maneuver, through sheer external force and strength, whereas a dragon style would rely more on *Qi*, or the projection of inner energy.

Kung fu (wushu) is an important highlighting element in contemporary Chinese culture and features in martial arts movies, such as the Oscar Award winning *Crouching Tiger, Hidden Dragon*.

功　夫

　　在西方，功夫被认为是中国的技击术；在中国，技击术通常被称为武术，指格斗的方法和套路，而功夫则主要指一个人在武艺方面所达到的造诣。与所有其他武术一样，中国功夫（武术）体现了自卫与健身的结合、技击之术与体育运动的结合、艺术和纪律的结合、哲学和生活方式的结合。

　　与中国文化的许多方面一样，武术的历史可以追溯到远古时期，有记录表明它至少始于商朝（前 1600 — 前 1046）。公元 500 年左右，中原少林寺的和尚们发明了一种武术形式，既可以锻炼身体，又可以保护自己不受强盗攻击。许多现代武术形式就是在少林武术的基础上直接发展起来的。如今武术的流派和套路共有一千多种。

　　道家强调气和练气功的重要性，对于功夫（武术）的发展做出了同样重要的贡献，因为武术要求习武者严格锻炼自己的身心，这正是道家的追求。为取得身心两方面的功夫，习武者须投入大量精力。功夫的不少套路都源自动物的动作，各种遮挡、攻击动作和姿式都模仿特定动物的举动。如标准武打招式之一的虎式可以靠纯外力断石，而龙式更多依靠运用内气。

　　功夫（武术）是彰显当代中国文化的一个很重要的部分，是武打片的主要内容，如奥斯卡获奖影片《卧虎藏龙》。

练武的僧人（时代图片供）

Lacquerware

Lacquerware derives its name from the raw lacquer that is a product of the lacquer tree, which is indigenous to China. The sap of the lacquer tree hardens when it comes into contact with the air, thus creating the distinctive luster or sheen of lacquerware.

Like many other kinds of art and craft from China, lacquerware has a long and distinguished history. A wood-based red lacquer bowl dates from about 6 000 years ago. The earliest lacquerware pieces were colored red or black, much like early Greek vases. During the Warring States (475BC – 221BC) and **Han dynasty** (206 BC – AD 220) periods, lacquer- ware was decorated with vivid patterns of animals and clouds.

现代漆雕花瓶

Prior to the invention of ink in China, lacquer was used for writing. A number of bamboo strips found in a Warring States period tomb in Henan province contain lists of buried items written in lacquer.

Among the most important cities producing lacquerware are Beijing, Fuzhou and Yangzhou. Beijing lacquerware typically carries anywhere from dozens to hundreds of layers of lacquer over its wooden base. These layers of lacquer can range to a thickness of 20 millimeters. Into these layers, artists carve designs to create complex images of landscapes filled with flowers, animals, and human figures.

漆　器

漆器得名于生漆。生漆出自漆树，漆树的原产地是中国。漆树的汁液一旦接触空气就开始变硬，这样就给漆器带来一层独特的色泽或光彩。

与中国其他许多工艺品一样，漆器有着悠久的历史。有一个出土的红漆木碗是大约六千年前制造的。最早的漆器都是红色或黑色的，很像早期的希腊花瓶。战国时期（前 475 – 前 221）和**汉朝**（前 206 – 220）生产的漆器上则绘有生动的动物和云彩花纹。

西汉时期的漆器

在墨发明之前，漆可以用来写字。河南省发掘的一座战国古墓里出土了一些竹简，上面所列的陪葬品名称就是用漆写的。

漆器最重要的产地是北京、福州和扬州。北京漆器的胎体上通常覆盖着几十到上百层漆，漆的厚度可达 20 毫米。艺术家们在漆层上雕出复杂的山水、花鸟和人物图案。

明代的漆器

97

Laotze (Lao Tzu)

Laotze, which means roughly "the old tutor" or "the old master", lived during the sixth century BC, and was a contemporary of **Confucius.** It was with Laotze that the philosophy of **Daoism** (Taoism) originated, as he is the reputed author of the *Dao De Jing (Tao Te Ching)*. According to legend, Laotze was the keeper of the archives at the imperial court. At the age of eighty, seeing the irrevokable decline of the Zhou court which he had been serving, and disillusioned that his teachings were being ignored, he resigned and traveled to the western border of China. At the border he was asked by the general guarding the border to write his teachings down in a book before leaving. The 5 000-word treatises he wrote became the central Daoist text, the *Daodejing*, which has been translated into many languages, almost as often as the Bible.

The teachings of Laotze can be contrasted with those of Confucius, with the two approaches offering distinct responses to life in China 2 500 years ago. Confucius emphasized

明·张路《老子骑牛图》

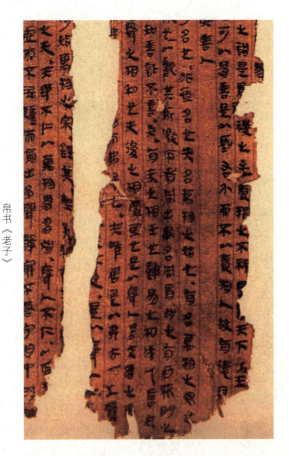

帛书《老子》

social relations, focusing on conduct and family relationships. Laotze, on the other hand, focused on the individual, offering a more mystical set of guidelines for living, and an emphasis on nature rather than society. Confucianism and Daoism can be considered the **Yin** and **Yang** of Chinese philosophy.

Laotze has also been compared with Socrates in his emphasis on the limitations of knowledge – both self knowledge and knowledge of the world. Both philosophers were wise because they knew what they did not know. Neither feared death. And both saw their role as guiding others on a search for truth. Laotze differed from Socrates, however, in his emphasis on seeking the way, or the *dao*, in nature, and by following intuition rather than rules in discovering and mastering one's self.

老子

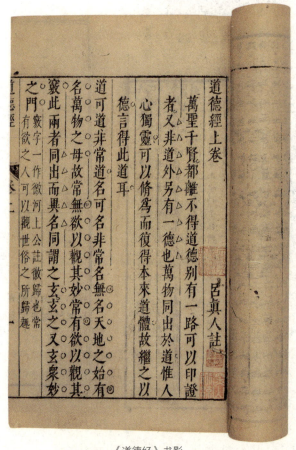

《道德经》书影

"老子",意思是"老夫子"或"老先生"。老子生活在公元前六世纪，与**孔子**同时代。**道家**哲学源自老子，因为据信他是《道德经》的作者。传说老子曾为朝廷管理文书档案。80岁时，他眼见自己所服务的周王朝在走向衰败，并因为自己的主张不被世人接受而产生幻灭感，于是辞官西行。路过边关，边关守将建议他在离去前把自己的教义写成书。老子所写的这本约五千字的书就是道家典籍的核心之作——《道德经》。此书被翻译成多种文字，译本的数量几乎与《圣经》一样多。

老子与孔子的教义可形成对比，他们从两个不同的角度，对两千五百年前的中国社会生活提出了自己的看法。孔子强调社会关系，关注行为操守和家庭关系。而老子侧重于个人，提出了一套更具神秘色彩的人生指导。老子注重自然而不是社会。儒家和道家可谓中国哲学里的**阴**与**阳**。

　　人们也常将老子和苏格拉底加以对比。两位学者都强调知识的局限性——包括关于自身和世界的知识。两位哲学家都很有智慧，因为他们知道自己不知道什么。二人都不惧怕死亡，并且都认识到自己扮演着引导他人寻求真理的角色。然而，他们也有不同之处。老子注重寻求自然中的道，并在发现和掌控自我时依靠直觉而非依靠规则。

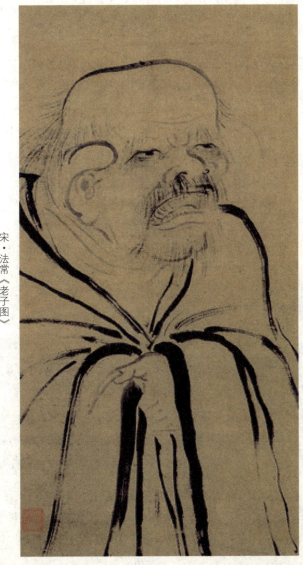

宋·法常《老子图》

Li Bai

Li Bai (Li Po, 701 – 762), along with **Du Fu**, is the best known of all Chinese poets, and perhaps the most beloved. If Du Fu is sometimes called the **Confucian** poet, Li Bai is identified as a **Daoist** poet, since his poems exhibit a spontaneous sense of freedom and a defiance of convention, as they also often celebrate nature. Often referred to as "the Immortal Poet", Li Bai wrote nearly one thousand poems. Among his most popular subjects are friendship, nature, and drinking either with friends or alone.

Like Du Fu, Li Bai has been a major influence on Chinese poets of succeeding generations, and he has also had a broader influence beyond China, including French and German poets of the nineteenth century and early twentieth century American poets. Li Bai is known in the west primarily through his influence on Ezra Pound, the American modernist poet. Here are some lines from Li Bai's "The River Merchant's Wife: a Letter", in Pound's translation:

At sixteen you departed,
You went into far Ku-to-en, by the river of swirling eddies,
And you have been gone five months.
The monkeys make sorrowful noise overhead.

宋·梁楷《李白行吟图》

You dragged your feet when you went out.

By the gate now, the moss is grown, the different mosses,

Too deep to clear them away!

The leaves fall early this autumn, in wind.

The paired butterflies are already yellow with August.

Over the grass in the West garden;

They hurt me. I grow older.

Li Bai, unlike Du Fu, achieved fame during his lifetime. And for all the energy and vitality of his poetry, there is also a deep core of loneliness, seen not only in "The River-Merchant's Wife", but also in poems such as "Drinking Alone with the Moon":

From a pot of wine among the flowers

I drank alone. There was no one with me –

Till, raising my cup, I asked the bright moon

To bring me my shadow and make us three.

Alas, the moon was unable to drink

And my shadow tagged me vacantly;

But still for a while I had these friends.

To cheer me through the end of spring...

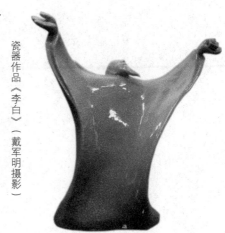

瓷器作品《李白》（戴军明摄影）

李 白

李白（701–762）和**杜甫**同是中国最著名的诗人，或许也是最受中国人喜爱的诗人。如果杜甫可被称为**儒家**诗人，那么李白就是**道家**诗人。他的诗有一种发自内心的自由感以及对常规的挑战，而且经常歌颂自然。李白常被称为"诗仙"，他创作的诗有近千首流传下来。在他的诗里，最常见的主题有友谊、自然和与朋友对饮或者独酌等。

与杜甫一样，李白对后世中国诗人产生了重要影响，其影响甚至超越中国，影响到包括19世纪的法国、德国诗人和20世纪早期的美国诗人。李白在美国为人所知，主要是通过其对美国诗人艾兹拉·庞德（Ezra Pound）的影响。以下是庞德所译的李白《长干行》一诗的部分内容：

> 十六君远行，瞿塘滟预堆。
>
> 五月不可触，猿鸣天上哀。
>
> 门前迟行迹，一一生绿苔。
>
> 苔深不能扫，落叶秋风早。
>
> 八月蝴蝶来，双飞西园草。
>
> 感此伤妾心，坐愁红颜老。

与杜甫不一样的是，李白生前就已成名。他的诗极具活力和生命力，但同时也有一种深深的孤独感。这种孤独感不仅表现在《长干行》里，还体现在《月下独酌》这样的诗中：

> 花间一壶酒，独酌无相亲。
>
> 举杯邀明月，对影成三人。
>
> 月既不解饮，影徒随我身。
>
> 暂伴月将影，行乐须及春。

清·苏六朋《太白醉酒图》

Lotus Flower

The Lotus is a much beloved flower in China, as indicated by the fondness of Chinese people for lotus flower paintings. The lotus is considered symbolic of a gentle person, elegant and beautiful even when surrounded by a dirty and unhealthy environment, in the manner of the lotus flower rises from the mud at the bottom of a pond. Symbolizing purity, the lotus is associated with summer, a time of beauty. In Chinese painting and poetry, ancient and modern, the lotus is presented as an image of beauty and freshness.

The root of the lotus contains a kind of very fine but extremely sinuous fibre, which remains intact and is visible when the root is broken into two halves. This strength is sometimes used by poets to symbolize the strong,

北京北海公园

unbreakable bond that exists between members of a family or between lovers.

The lotus is also a common symbol in **Buddhism**, where it represents sanctity. Many representations of the Buddha show him sitting on a lotus flower, often in meditation. The golden lotus mentioned in Buddhist scriptures, especially the Lotus Sutra, represents the attainment of enlightenment. The lotus sutra is the most popular scripture of Mahayana Buddhism, the form most popular in China, which emphasizes the salvation of all living beings in a spirit of compassion. It teaches that making holy images is an act of great merit and helps a person achieve enlightenment, the goal of Buddhism.

明·陈洪绶《荷花图》

莲 花

　　莲花深受中国人的喜爱。中国人非常喜欢画有莲花的画。莲花被视为君子的象征，君子即使身处污秽、不健康的环境，也洁身自好，就像莲花，出淤泥而不染，优雅而美丽。莲花象征纯洁，是代表美丽夏季的花。在中国画和诗歌里，不论是古代还是现代，莲花都被描绘成美和清新的形象。

　　莲藕里有一种非常细但极为坚韧的纤维，藕即使折断，这种纤维也不容易断，并且可以被看见，因此有"藕断丝连"的说法。有时，诗人用这种力量来象征家庭成员或恋人间坚强和牢不可破的纽带。

中国传统年画《莲年有余》(时代图片供)

荷塘幽梦（朱绛摄影）

　　莲花也是**佛教**中常见的象征，代表圣洁。许多画像和雕塑都表现佛
祖端坐在莲花上，往往在冥思。金莲是达到涅槃的象征，在佛教经典，
特别是《妙法莲花经》（简称《法华经》）中被多次提及。《法华经》强调
慈悲为怀，普渡众生，是中国最流行的佛教支派——大乘佛教流传最广
的经文。它教导人们，修筑佛像是极大的功德，有助于人们到达佛教的
目标——涅槃。

宋·佚名《太液荷风图》

Ming Dynasty

The Ming dynasty (1368 – 1644) was one of the greatest dynasties in China's history. The last native Han-led dynasty, the Ming dynasty was between the Mongol-led Yuan (1206 – 1368) dynasty and the **Qing dynasty** (1616 – 1911), which was led by the Manchus. Its capital in Beijing, the Ming ruled over a vast kingdom with a million-man army and a vast military. During the Ming dynasty, mariners under the order of the **emperor** undertook seven long voyages across the Indian Ocean, which made the Ming more influential abroad than were previous Chinese dynasties.

Among the many accomplishments of the Ming emperors was the development of the legal code, which was enlarged and improved to be more comprehensive, more intelligible, and more equitable than the previous code. The new legal code placed significant emphasis on family relations, based in large part on Confucian precepts.

The Ming was among the most prosperous of China's dynasties. Developments in agriculture and advances in science fueled that prosperity, and the production of porcelain and textiles flourished. Among its major contributions were its famous blue-on-white **porcelain** wares and the elegantly crafted wooden **Ming furniture** both of which remain popular around the world to this day.

The Ming also made significant improvements to the **Great Wall**, which was enlarged and repaired with redesigned watchtowers and the placement of cannons in strategic positions. Known for a complex and intricate government that established firm control throughout the vast country, it was this same intricacy and complexity that led to the Ming's decline.

明 朝

　　明朝（1368 — 1644）是中国历史上最伟大的朝代之一。它是汉族人统治的最后一个朝代，处在蒙古族人建立的元朝（1206 — 1368）和满族人建立的**清朝**（1616 — 1911）之间。明朝定都北京，疆域辽阔，拥有强大的军事力量。明代，**皇帝**曾命航海家七次横穿印度洋，这使明朝在国外产生了比前朝更大的影响。

　　明朝皇帝的众多成就之一就是推动了律法的发展。法律条文得到扩充，更加全面、易懂、公正。新律法主要以儒家思想为依据，更加注重家庭关系。

　　明代是中国历史上最繁荣的朝代之一。农业和科技的发展促进了社会的繁荣，陶瓷和纺织品制造业兴旺发达。其主要贡献包括至今全世界仍然流行的青花**瓷器**和工艺典雅的**明式木质家具**。

　　明朝还大规模重修了**长城**，加固、延长并重新设计了烽火台，在战略要点上安置了大炮。明朝以政府机构设置繁杂、统治森严而闻名，但这种复杂的政府机构设置和严酷的统治却加速了这个王朝的衰亡。

郑和下西洋的船队

Ming Furniture

The **Ming dynasty** is renowned for many things, not the least of which is the gracefully beautiful furniture that was created during its reign. Often completely unornamented, Ming dynasty furniture exhibits a perfection of line and an elegance of form unique in its austere beauty. The precious woods used to construct Ming furniture were typically left unlacquered, unlike furniture from the **Qing dynasty** (1616 – 1911).

Ming furniture is constructed with complex joinery without the use of nails or glue. The pieces are held together with elaborate mitre, mortise, and tenon joints, which enables them to be dissembled readily, of great importance for their original Chinese mandarin owners, who were obligated to move on a regular basis. Most Ming furniture was made from dense tropical hardwoods, called "hong mu", which was notable for its striking color and grain. One of the most popular woods and highly sought after today is scented rosewood. Though other woods were used, such as the dark and striking red sandalwood, as well as wenge and elmwood, scented rosewood is the wood most frequently seen in museum quality Ming dynasty furniture. Different woods and

明代的床

striking design variations give each piece a unique character.

Ming furniture mingles form with function. The furniture was designed to reflect and dramatize the purposes for which it was designed. Ming beds, for example, were considered miniature houses with their covered tops and semi-enclosed sides. Ming tables were designed for the use of scholars to write and paint as well as to dine. And Ming chairs were designed less for comfort than for elegance of design and strength of structure. Chairs were placed and positioned according to the rank of the sitters. Where you sat indicated who you were.

明代的黄花梨柜子

明代家具

　　明朝因许多东西而闻名，其中很重要的一样东西就是那时制作的典雅、美观的家具。明代家具常不带任何装饰，线条流畅，造型优雅，展示了一种独特的质朴美。明代家具所用的珍贵的木头上通常不上漆，这与**清朝**（1616 — 1911）家具不同。

　　明代家具是用复杂的榫卯工艺组装起来的，不用钉子或胶。部件用

明代的家具陈设

精细的对角和榫卯结合在一起，使家具容易拆卸。这对拥有这些家具但定期需要搬家的明朝官员非常重要。明代家具的制作多采用产自热带、木质细密的红木，这种木材以色泽和纹路美观闻名，其中最受欢迎并且至今仍备受追捧的一种木头是黄花梨。尽管人们也用其他木头制造家具，如深色紫檀木、鸡翅木和榆木，但黄花梨木的明代家具最具收藏价值。不同的材质和别出心裁的设计式样，使每一件家具都各具特色。

明代家具集式样与功能于一体。家具的设计彰显了其设计意图。如明代的床被设计成缩微房屋式样，床上有顶，床周半封闭。明代的桌子既可作为学者写字绘画的书桌，也可用作餐桌。明朝椅子的设计，更注重其外观的典雅和结构的力度，而不是其舒适度。椅子是根据坐椅子的人的地位摆放的，你坐在哪里就表明你地位如何。

明代的椅子

Monkey King

The Monkey King, Sun Wukong, the central character in the Chinese classical novel *Journey to the West*, is among the most popular and beloved character in all of Chinese literature. The Monkey King is ruler and sage, warrior, priest, and magician rolled into one, and disguised as a monkey. Possibly based upon a monkey character, Hanuman, in the ancient Hindu epic, the *Ramayana*, the Monkey King undergoes a series of wild and wonderful adventures, as he accompanies the monk Xuan Zang to India to bring back Buddhist scriptures.

According to the legends, Wukong was born from a stone, which symbolizes his strength and indestructibility. He was a brave young monkey when, saddened by the thought of his mortality, he went looking for immortal beings and eventually found the Patriarch Subodhi, who took him as a disciple. Under the Patriarch's direction, the Monkey King acquires immortality, learns to change his appearance and form, and to change the appearance of others as well.

In the novel, through acts of heroism, cunning, and skill, he helps Xuan Zang succeed in his quest and accomplish his mission. In modern China he is regarded as a figure to emulate, and was frequently cited by Chairman Mao Zedong as an example of fearless and successful achievement. His character has inspired many modern adaptations of the original classic novel, including characters on a number of television series, comic and dramatic films, novels, and also adaptations of his story, including a translation of *Journey to the West* entitled *Monkey*, in his honor, and even exists in a version as a Microsoft XP Office Assistant.

美 猴 王

美猴王即孙悟空，他是中国古典小说《**西游记**》里的核心人物，是中国文学里最受欢迎和喜爱的角色之一。美猴王集统治者、圣贤（齐天大圣）、勇士、僧侣、魔术师为一身，以猴子的形象出现。其人物创作很可能借鉴了古印度史诗《罗摩衍那》中神猴哈努曼（*Hanuman*）的形象。美猴王伴随玄奘和尚西去印度求取佛经，经历了一系列坎坷而辉煌的冒险历程。

传说孙悟空是从石头里生出来的，这象征着他的强大力量和坚不可摧。当他还只是一只勇敢的年轻猴子时，想到自己难免一死，非常沮丧，于是开始寻求长生不老之法。最终他找到了菩提老祖，并成为其门徒。在菩提老祖的教导下，他得到了不死之身，学会了七十二变，并能改变他人他物的外表。

在小说里，孙悟空借助其勇敢、机智和武艺，帮助玄奘成功取到真经，顺利完成了使命。在当代中国，他被视为值得效仿的人物，毛泽东主席曾经常提到他，以他作为英勇无畏、取得胜利的例子。美猴王的形象激发人们对《西游记》这一古典小说进行了多次现代版的改编，包括好几部电视连续剧、动画片、戏剧片、小说和译本。《西游记》一个英文本的译名就是*Monkey*（猴），可见人们对他有多喜爱。甚至 Microsoft XP Office 的一个 office 助手形象也是孙悟空。

京剧中的孙悟空（时代图片供）

Mountains

Mountains cover two thirds of China, which possesses more of the world's tallest peaks than any other country, including the world summit – Mt. Qomolangma in Tibet. Mountains often appear in Chinese landscape paintings, and are typically portrayed as grand and majestic. When humans are included in paintings of Chinese mountains, they are usually tiny in comparison to the mountains, suggesting how the grandeur and immensity of nature dwarfs human life. Mountains are frequently mentioned by Chinese poets in their poetry, including **Li Bai**, and are especially important in the writings of **Daoist** poets and philosophers.

A number of mountains are considered sacred, with different peaks

云雾笼罩的黄山莲花峰（刘鹏建摄影）

安徽齐云山风光 (朱　绛摄影)

achieving sacred status with Buddhists and Daoists. Among the most famous are Mount Tai in Shandong Province, which has been considered a sacred site since the **Qin Dynasty** (221 BC – 206 BC), Mount Hua, in Shaanxi Province, whose name means "flower", because its five peaks resemble a **lotus flower** in bloom, and Mount Song in Henan Province, where the Shaolin Monastery, the birthplace of **Zen Buddhism** in China, is located. Also important was the Wutai Mountain, which has more than seventy temples and over twenty thousand Buddhist statues.

Among the best known mountains in China is the Huangshan mountain range, in the eastern part of the country. An area that includes hot springs and natural pools, it is famous for its scenic beauty, which has often served as subject and source of inspiration for Chinese painters. With a number of its mountain peaks above cloud level, views from its heights are known for their extraordinary light effects.

山

　　山覆盖了中国三分之二的土地面积。中国拥有的世界高峰比其他任何一个国家都多，其中包括位于西藏的世界最高峰珠穆朗玛峰（Mt. Qomolangma）。高大雄伟的山经常出现在中国的风景画里。当人出现在这些画里时，人与山相比显得很微小，从而展示了自然的壮观、浩瀚和人生的渺小。山常常出现在包括**李白**在内的中国诗人的诗和词人的词里，在**道家**诗人和哲学家的著作中，山更是扮演了重要角色。

　　在人们心目中，有一些山是神圣的。不同的山峰在佛教和道教中分别享有神圣的地位。最著名的山包括山东的泰山、陕西的华山、河南的嵩山。泰山自**秦朝**（前 221 — 前 206）就被视为神圣之地；华山的"华"通"花"，因其五座山峰犹如一朵盛开的**莲花**而得名；嵩山是中国佛教**禅**宗的发源地少林寺的所在地。此外，五台山也很重要，山上有七十余座

珠穆朗玛峰（时代图片供）

寺庙和两万余尊佛像。

　　中国最著名的山当中还有黄山。黄山位于中国东部，该地区有众多温泉和湖泊，因美景如画而著称，常激发中国画家的创作灵感，成为他们所描绘的对象。黄山有多座高于云海的山峰，峰顶的风景以其非凡的光线效果而闻名。

释一智《黄山天都峰》

Opera
(Beijing Opera)

Beijing opera, still known as Peking opera, is the national opera of China. A repository of Chinese culture, it is known for its rich vein of traditional stories, its exquisite costumes, elegant gestures, and acrobatic fight scenes, accompanied by traditional Chinese music and singing.

Beijing opera was performed mostly on stages fit up in the streets, at markets, teahouses, and temple courtyards. Singers developed a sharp style of singing that could carry through the noise of street life. The orchestra played loud, and costumes were vivid and dramatic. Over its more than two hundred years of history, Beijing opera underwent a variety of developments, picking up the influence of local opera traditions of other cities. It became a more popular form of entertainment for the common people during the reigns of the **Qing Emperor** Qianlong and the Qing Empress Dowager Cixi.

Incorporating traditional styles of acting absorbed from the history of Chinese drama, Beijing opera possesses a distinctive liveliness, with colorful, fast-paced scenes based on ancient Chinese myths, legends, and fables. Its dramatic action is highly stylized, as with 26 distinct ways to laugh and 39 ways to manipulate the 20 types of beards, etc. Performers' roles are divided into four categories: male (*sheng*), female (*dan*), special male (*jing*), and clown (*chou*). Male and female roles, traditionally all performed by men, are subdivided into roles for old men with beards and roles for young men without beards, including the flirtatious yet witty female and the lady of propriety, etc.

The music for Peking opera is performed by an orchestra arranged in two parts: a percussion section of gongs and drums, which play introductory and interval music, and a melodic section of strings and wind instruments, which accompanies the singing.

戏剧（京剧）

京剧是中国的国剧，蕴涵了深厚的中国文化，讲述不计其数的传统故事，展示精美的服装、优雅的舞姿、精湛的武打，同时伴有传统中国音乐和唱腔。

京剧最初主要在大街和集市上、茶馆和寺庙的院子里搭起舞台进行表演。演唱者发明了一种有着激扬风格的唱腔，可力透街市生活的嘈杂。乐队伴奏的声音很响，服装艳丽而有戏剧效果。京剧在其两百多年的历史中，经历了多个发展阶段，吸收了其他地方传统戏剧的影响。在清朝乾隆皇帝和慈禧太后统治期间，京剧发展成为群众最喜闻乐见的戏剧形式。

京剧从中国戏剧史中吸取了传统的表演风格，散发出独具特色的勃勃生机。剧情取材于中国神话、传说和寓言，舞台色彩斑斓，布景变换节奏快。表演动作高度程式化，如有 26 种不同笑法、20 种胡须及 39 种操控胡须的方法等。演出角色分为四类，包括生（男）、旦（女）、净（绘有花脸的特殊角色）和丑（小丑）。这些角色又被细分为有胡须的老生和无胡须的小生，还有俏皮的花旦和端庄的青衣等。

演奏京剧音乐的乐队分为两组，一组使用锣鼓等打击乐器，演奏开场和过场；另一组使用管弦乐器为演唱者伴奏。

京剧《贵妃醉酒》(时代图片供)

Peking Duck

Peking Duck, more accurately Peking Roast Duck, is among the best known and most popular of Chinese dishes. Peking Roast Duck is served in numerous restaurants throughout China, but the most famous establishment is Quanjude Roast Duck Restaurant in Beijing which has served this splendid dish for well over a hundred years. And although the history of Peking Roast Duck dates to the Yuan dynasty (1206 – 1368), it became immensely popular with the reigning **Ming dynasty** royalty in the fifteenth century.

Among the most critical procedures of serving Peking Duck is to present thin slices of meat which needs careful study. One way is to present thin slices of the crisp skin and then the thin slices of the meat onto plates, and another is to present every thin slice of meat with skin attached. Traditionally, Peking Duck is served in three courses: first, various cold or hot dishes made of such things as duck liver, duck heart and duck stomach, and the web of duck feet; second, placing thin strips of duck meat on one or another type of thin Chinese pancake, adding bits of onion and special sauces, rolling it up, and eating it by hand; second, and finally, after finishing the meat, having Peking duck soup broth made from the bones.

One additional and different understanding of Peking duck follows from the way a Peking duck is stuffed before cooking which is known as a stuffed duck. China, Japan, and some other Asian countries follow a system of "stuffing" students with knowledge and information regardless of method and efficiency in teaching, to cram them for tests. This is referred to as "Peking duck-style" education. More often, however, the cramming is of the gustatory variety.

北京烤鸭

北京烤鸭

北京烤鸭是最著名和最受欢迎的中国菜之一，在中国各地的餐馆里都可吃到，不过最有名的要数北京的全聚德烤鸭店，该店制作这一美味佳肴已有百余年的历史。尽管北京烤鸭的历史可以追溯到元代（1206 — 1368），它却是在 15 世纪的**明朝**皇族中才变得大受欢迎。

北京烤鸭这道菜最重要的一道工序是片鸭。片鸭也有讲究：一种方法是先片酥脆的鸭皮，然后把剩下的鸭肉也片成片，一起摆上餐盘；一种方法是每片都带皮带肉。传统上，北京烤鸭主要有三种吃法：一是把鸭肝、鸭心、鸭胗、鸭掌等做成凉菜或热菜吃；二是把片成薄片的烤鸭肉放在一种薄面饼上，加上一些大葱丝，蘸上特制的面酱，卷起来用手拿着吃；三是吃完鸭肉后喝用鸭骨架熬的鸭汤。

北京鸭在饲养期间，人们会往其胃里填塞大量食物，叫填鸭。"填鸭"还有另一种含义：中国、日本和亚洲其他一些国家，把教学不讲方法效率，硬给学生脑中"填塞"各种知识和信息，以应对考试，称为"填鸭式"教育。当然，"填塞"更多还是用于餐饮上。

卷烤鸭

125

Phoenix

The phoenix is a mythical bird. In western mythology it consumes itself with fire every five hundred years, with another phoenix emanating from its ashes, and is thus associated with immortality. In Chinese mythology, it does not undergo this cycle of rebirth. The Chinese phoenix has the head of the golden pheasant, the beak of the parrot, the body of the mandarin duck, the wings of the roc, the legs of the crane, and the feathers of the peacock. The phoenix has long been highly regarded in China, symbolizing beauty, harmony, luck, female energy, and the Empress, as the **dragon** represents the **Emperor.** And as the Emperor sleeps on a dragon bed and sits on a dragon throne, so the Empress is carried in a "phoenix carriage" and covered with a "phoenix canopy".

Together with its dragon counterpart, the phoenix serves in classical literature and art as a metaphor for talent, beauty, and virtue, as well as for matrimonial unity and harmony. Dragon and phoenix dances are popular at many Chinese festivals, and dragon and phoenix decorations are ubiquitous on Chinese clothing, pottery, and numerous other everyday objects, past and present.

In the realm of art, the phoenix creates excitement and inspiration, with a wide capacity for vision.

凤凰图样

When a phoenix is used as a house decoration, it suggests auspiciousness and peace. Jewelry decorated with the phoenix emblem mark the wearer as a person of importance and high moral values. When depictions of the phoenix are found on tombs and grave markers, it typically indicates that a royal female is buried below.

宫殿石阶上雕刻的凤凰

凤　凰

中国画《凤凰》

　　凤凰是神话中的一种鸟。在西方神话中，凤凰每 500 年将自己焚毁于大火中，然后灰烬中会飞出另一只凤凰，因此凤凰代表不朽。在中国传统神话中，没有凤凰 500 年自焚后重生的传说。中国的凤凰是一种祥瑞之鸟，它有锦鸡的头，鹦鹉的喙，鸳鸯的身子，大鹏的翅膀，鹤的腿和孔雀的羽毛。凤凰在中国长期受到珍重，是美丽、和谐、幸运、女性力量和皇后的象征；与之对应，**龙象征皇帝**。皇帝卧龙床，坐龙椅，皇后则乘凤舆出行，用凤盖遮荫。

在古典文学和艺术作品中，凤凰与龙一起，用来比喻才华、美丽、美德以及婚姻的和谐美满。龙凤舞是中国很多节日里一个受欢迎的节目。从古至今，龙凤装饰在中国服装、陶器和无数其他日用品中随处可见。

在艺术领域，凤凰引发激情和灵感，可产生丰富的视觉效果。房屋上装饰的凤凰图案寓意吉祥和太平。带有凤凰形象的首饰，则显示佩戴者是品格高尚的贵人。如果发现坟墓或墓碑上刻有凤凰形象，则通常表示此处埋葬的是一位皇族女性。

清·任颐《朱竹凤凰图》

Pipa

The pipa is a four-stringed lute with a pear-shaped body of different sizes and which include differing numbers of frets, as few as ten and as many as thirty. The pipa's frets are made of wood, ivory, or jade, with its strings made of silk. The pipa's history is a long one, being mentioned in texts dating from the **Han dynasty** (206 BC – AD 220). Since the **Tang dynasty** (618 – 907), the pipa has been among the most popular of Chinese musical instruments, maintaining its appeal as both a chamber instrument and as a solo instrument.

The popularity of the pipa can be compared to that of the Spanish or classical guitar. Both instruments are plucked with the fingernails, with the pipa producing a sound resembling that of a harpsichord. They have three open-string tunings in common: A, D, and E. Performers on the two instruments share some plucking techniques, including rapidly wheeling the fingers of the right hand over a string to create a sustained tremolo effect.

Contemporary professional players of the pipa perform both traditional pipa music and modern compositions written for the instrument. They also play music of other cultures, including western music, both popular and classical. The contemporary performers Wu Man and Liu Fang play music that embraces a variety of world music, including the Indian music of Ravi Shankar, as well as music from Korea, Japan, Ethiopia, Europe, and the United States. Both of these artists also play traditional Chinese music, such as "Dance of the Yi People", a popular favorite often required by conservatory juries of prospective pipa students.

琵 琶

琵琶

琵琶有四根琴弦和一个梨形琴身，规格大小不一，品数也不一，少则 10 个，多者达 30 个。琵琶的品用木头、象牙或玉石磨制而成，琴弦是丝制的。琵琶是一种有着悠久历史的乐器，在**汉朝**（前 206 — 220）书籍中就有记载。自**唐朝**（618 — 907）以来，琵琶成为中国最受欢迎的乐器之一，既可用作室内乐器，又可用作独奏乐器。

琵琶受欢迎的程度堪与西班牙吉他或古典吉他相比。二者都用指甲拨奏，琵琶的声音近似拨弦键琴。它们有三个相同的空弦调阶：A、D 和 E。两种乐器的演奏者也使用一些相同的弹拨技法，包括用右手手指快速来回拨动琴弦，制造出持续的颤音效果。

当代专业琵琶演奏者既弹奏传统琵琶曲目，也弹奏专为琵琶创作的现代乐曲。他们还演奏其他文化的音乐，包括西方流行音乐和古典音乐。当代琵琶演奏家吴蛮和刘芳演奏的音乐作品来自世界各地，包括拉维·香卡的印度音乐以及韩国、日本、埃塞俄比亚、欧洲和美国音乐。他们也弹奏传统中国乐曲，如《彝族舞曲》，这是一首音乐学院老师通常要求考生弹奏的考试曲目。

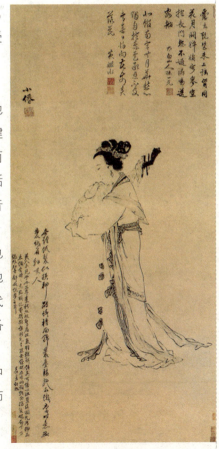

明·吴伟《琵琶美人图》

Porcelain

For over 1 800 years, Chinese potters produced masterpieces of porcelain ceramic ware, commonly known simply as "fine china", in an amazing variety of shapes, colors, and decorative styles. Among the best known and most appreciated in the west are **Tang dynasty** (618 – 907) porcelain pieces – tomb figures, horses, camels, soldiers, and courtesans, among others. Equally prized are the fine designs of flowers and animals enlivened by special effects of "partridge feather", "hare's fur", and "oil spot", used on white, ivory, willow, celadon and shades of blue porcelain produced during the **Song dynasty** (960 – 1279). The Chinese were able to create such astonishing ceramic and porcelain works due to their understanding of how to control kiln temperatures and to their extensive knowledge of glazes, including how to mix them to create unusual effects of color.

Celadon and black porcelain became popular during the **Han dynasty** (206 BC – AD 220). During the Tang era, porcelain wares were more commonly used, and both celadon and white porcelain wares were big and used mostly as bowls, plates, vases, pots, etc. During the Song period, porcelain modulated from a utilitarian product to one with strong aesthetic appeal. It was during this time that porcelain became a collectible item. Song dynasty porcelain is noted for its elegance, delicacy, and graceful appearance. The more elaborately decorated porcelain in popular patterns of blue on white that were developed during the **Ming** and **Qing dynasties** from the 14th through the 19th centuries remain popular today.

瓷　器

　　一千八百多年以来，中国陶工生产出了形式多样、色彩丰富、装饰风格各异的陶瓷杰作，它们一般被称为"细瓷"。在西方，最为著名和最受人喜爱的一种瓷器是**唐朝**（618 — 907）的三彩陶瓷——陶人俑、马俑、驼俑、士兵俑、舞伎俑等。同样珍贵的是**宋朝**（960 — 1279）生产的白瓷、象牙瓷、柳斗纹瓷、青瓷及天青色瓷器等都很出名，瓷器上用鹧鸪斑、兔毫、油滴等特殊工艺绘制的花草和动物栩栩如生。中国工匠由于懂得如何控制瓷窑温度，掌握了全面的上釉知识，包括用混合釉彩制造特殊色彩，因此他们生产出了令人叹为观止的陶瓷制品。

　　汉朝（前206 — 220）流行青瓷和黑瓷。唐朝，瓷器更为普及，无论青瓷还是白瓷器形大多为碗、盘、瓶、壶等。在宋朝，部分瓷器逐渐从实用的产品转变为极具观赏价值的艺术品，开始被人们收藏。宋瓷以典雅、精致和优美的外观而闻名。**明清**时期（14 至 19 世纪）发明的青花瓷上绘有更为精细的纹饰，流行至今。

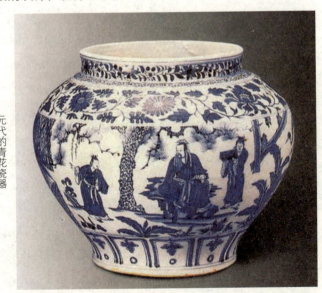

元代的青花瓷器

Qin Dynasty

Under the leadership of Ying Zheng (259 BC – 210 BC), the Qin king, the widespread regions of China were united politically for the first time in the country's history, which prior to the Qin, had been known as the period of the Warring States. The English word *China* is thought to have derived from the Latin word *Chin* in Marco Polo's time, and Chin initially referred to none other country than Qin, After unifying the whole country, Ying Zheng, named himself the First **Emperor** (Shi Huangdi), and instituted a number of changes, including dividing up the country into 36 regions, each with a governor, military commander, and imperial inspector. Families were organized into groups of five and ten households, which monitored the behavior of individuals within the group. Rewards and punishments were put in place to bolster a Legalist form of government, which the emperor established.

The many accomplishments of the Qin include standardizing the writing system of the country, the currency, and the weights and measures, and buidling chariot roads from the capital to various parts of the country. These roads were of the same width, much like today's expressway. Among the most ambitious of Qin projects was the building of a **Great Wall** to protect against invaders from the north. A less salutary act was the burning of thousands of books that were deemed detrimental to the emporer's rule and the execution of many **Confucian** scholars who were considered political dissidents along with some alchemists. When Qin Shi Huang died, he was buried in a lavish tomb he had built for himself 30 kilometers to the east of Xi'an, complete with an army of life-size terracotta **warriors**. In 1974, just a few kilometers from Qin Shi Huang's tomb, farmers stumbled upon the remains of these of terra-cotta warrior figures that had been buried to accompany the emperor into the afterlife. More than 8 000 terra-cotta warriors and horses have been found to date, along with innumerable bronze weapons and chariots, etc. in three major pit digging sites.

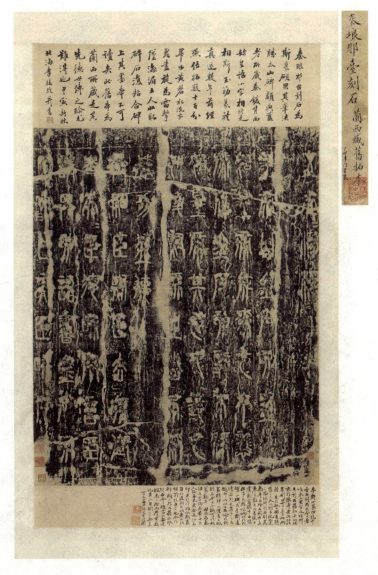

秦琅琊台刻石拓本

秦　朝

　　在秦王嬴政（前 259 — 前 210）的领导下，中国辽阔的疆域首次在政治上得到统一。在秦朝统一之前，中国处于战国时期。据说 China"中国"这个词源于马可波罗时代的拉丁词 Chin，而 Chin 最初指的正是"秦"。y嬴政统一全国后，自封为始**皇帝**（秦始皇），并实施了一系列改革，包括将全国划分为 36 个郡，每郡任命一个郡守、郡尉和监察使；将人民组织起来，每五户组成伍，每十户组成什，各伍各什的成员互相监督；赏罚到人，以巩固皇帝创建的法制政权。

　　秦朝有很多重大成就，包括统一全国的文字、货币、度量衡，修筑从京城通向四面八方的驰道，这些驰道的宽度相同，类似今天的高速公路。

秦俑博物馆

最具雄心的工程是修筑**长城**以抵御北方的侵略。另一项不那么光彩的举动是他下令焚烧了成千上万册被视为可能对统治者不利的书，处死了几百名被视为持异见者的**儒家**学者以及一些方术之士。秦始皇死后，被葬在西安以东 30 公里处一座他为自己修筑的奢华陵墓里，陵墓周围埋葬着由真人大小的陶**兵马俑**组成的军团。1974 年，在距秦始皇陵几公里处，几位农民不经意间发现了这些伴随秦始皇进入地下的陶兵马俑。迄今在三处主要发掘坑里已发现八千余座陶兵马俑及无数青铜兵器和战车等。

秦兵马俑

Qing Dynasty

The Qing dynasty (1616 – 1911) was the last of the Chinese dynastic empires, in this case, Manchus controlled the country. During the reigns of the three early Qing **emperors**, Kangxi (1662 – 1722), Yongzheng (1722 – 1736), and Qianlong (1736 – 1796), China experienced peace and prosperity. These leaders were not only strong military leaders and political rulers, they were also scholars who read and wrote poetry and valued the classics.

The Manchu Qing emperors preserved their cultural identity by outlawing intermarriage with Han ethnic group and by forbidding the Han to travel to Manchuria or to learn the Manchus' language. Kangxi reunified China by forcing the Ming remnants on the island of Taiwan to surrender and set up the Qing empire by conquering the rebel nomadic tribes of Mongolia that had occupied Tibet and establishing the central government's direct control over Tibet. His agricultural program of flood control was based on **Confucian** precepts, and he was an avid supporter of Confucian schools.

Kangxi's grandson, Qianlong, continued to pacify the southwest and northwest frontiers, laying the territorial ground work of China as a unified multi-ethnic country. Reputed to have composed more than 100 000 poems, Qianlong was a connoisseur of painting and **calligraphy.** Under his reign China prospered, remaining a well-organized, efficient, and extremely wealthy country.

Like its **Ming dynastic** predecessor, the Qing dynasty is known for its fine furniture, more elaborate than the simple Ming style, and for its beautiful porcelain ceramic ware.

清 朝

清乾隆坐像

清朝（1616 —1911）是中国最后一个王朝，由满族统治。清朝前期三位**皇帝**康熙（1662 —1722）、雍正（1722 —1736）和乾隆（1736 —1796）在位期间，中国社会国泰民安，繁荣富强。他们不仅是杰出的军事家和政治家，也是喜读诗书、擅长写作、珍重经典的学者。

满清皇帝禁止满汉通婚，禁止汉族人进入满洲和学习满文，以此维持满族文化。康熙通过迫降台湾岛上的明朝残余势力，重新统一了中国；他还征服了占据西藏的蒙古反叛游牧部落并建立了中央政府对西藏的直接管辖，确立了清帝国的版图。他在儒家观念的基础上制定了治理洪水、发展农业的方针，同时大力支持儒学。

康熙的孙子乾隆进一步平定了西南、西北边疆，奠定了中国统一的多民族国家的疆界基础。乾隆据称创作了十万余首诗，他还是一位**书法**和绘画鉴赏家。他在位期间，中国繁荣昌盛，社会秩序井然，国富民强。

与之前的**明朝**一样，清代也以精美家具闻名，清式家具比风格简洁的明式家具繁复。同时，清代的瓷器也同样享有盛名。

清康熙年间的太师椅

Renminbi

Renminbi, also known as *yuan*, is the official currency of China issued by the People's Bank of China, the monetary authority of the PRC. Renminbi, which is often abbreviated to RMB and is given the Latinized ¥ as its symbol, means "the people's currency". Renminbi was first issued in 1948 when the People's Bank of China was established. In 1955 a new set of Renminbi was issued to replace the first set at the rate of 1 new *yuan* to 10 000 old *yuan*.

Current bills range from the largest at 100 Yuan to the smallest at 1 *fen*, which is also issued as a coin, and which is valued at one-hundredth, or one percent, of 1 Yuan.

The word "*yuan*" in Chinese means "first" or "beginning". It is said that "*yuan*" came to be a currency unit in the **Ming Dynasty** when foreign silver dollars were introduced into China. Silver dollars were round and each coin is called one Yuan (meaning "round") which is both the name and the unit of the currency. Later on, for the sake of writing convenience, people started to use its homophone "*yuan*" (meaning "first") to replace Yuan (meaning "round"). The Japanese *yen* and the Korean *won* are cognate with the Chinese *yuan*. One of the key economic issues of the early twenty-first century is the extent to which the *yuan* should be revalued and allowed to fluctuate in tandem with other currencies, such as the Japanese yen or the US dollar.

人　民　币

　　人民币也称为"元"，是中国的官方货币，由中华人民共和国的金融管理机构中国人民银行发行。人民币的意思是"人民的货币"，常被简写为 RMB，代号是拉丁字母￥。第一套人民币是 1948 年中国人民银行成立时发行的。1955 年发行了第二套人民币，1 元新币值 10 000 元旧币。

　　现行纸币最大面值 100 元，最小面值 1 分。不仅有 1 分的纸币，还有 1 分的硬币。1 分是 1 元的百分之一。

　　"元"的意思是"首"、"始"。"元"作货币单位据说是从**明朝**开始的。当时外国的银元开始传入中国，银元是圆形的，一枚称为一圆，"圆"既是货币名称，又是货币单位。后来为了书写方便，人们就用同音的"元"代替了"圆"。日本的日元（yen）和韩国的韩元（won）是中国元的同源词。21 世纪初的一个重大经济问题就是，应在多大程度上重新确定人民币的价值，并允许与日元、美元等其他货币一起浮动。

人民币

Rivers

There are more than 1 500 rivers in China, with the most famous being the **Yangtze** and the Yellow rivers. The Yangze is the longest river in China with a full length of 6 200 kilometers, and the third longest in the world, after the Nile and the Amazon. The Yangtze and Yellow rivers both flow east and empty in the Pacific Ocean. With these and many other large river systems, China is rich in water-power resources and leads the world in potential for hydro-electric power.

The Yangtze, known as the "golden waterway", is a major transportation artery that links east and west with its excellent channels benefiting navigation. In the middle and lower reaches of this great river are important agricultural regions with abundant rainfall and fertile soil.

The Yellow River valley is considered one of the birthplaces of Chinese civilization. It is the second largest in China, flowing more than 5 000 kilometers.

In addition to these great rivers China also contains the world's longest and oldest man-made waterway, the Beijing-Hangzhou Grand Canal, with a total length of 1 794 kilometers. Taking more than 1 700 years to construct, beginning in 486 BC during the **Zhou dynasty** (1046 BC – 256 BC). Flowing north to south, it starts in Beijing in the north and ends in the southern city of Hangzhou.

河　流

　　中国有一千五百多条江河，其中最著名的是**长江**和黄河。长江是中国最长的河流，全长 6 200 多公里，也是仅次于尼罗河和亚马孙河的世界第三大河流。长江和黄河均自西向东流入太平洋。它们及其他的大型水系使中国拥有了丰富的水力资源和世界领先的水电潜能。

　　被称为"黄金水道"的长江是横贯东西的交通动脉，为便利的航运提供了优良的水道，在这条大河的中下游地区是重要的农业区，雨量丰沛，土壤肥沃。

　　黄河流域被视为中华文明发祥地之一。黄河是中国的第二大河流，绵延 5 464 公里。

　　除这些大河外，中国还拥有世界最长和最古老的人工水道——京杭大运河，全长 1 794 公里，始建于公元前 486 年的**周朝**（前 1046 —前 256），前后共修建了 1 700 余年。大运河自北向南，北起北京，终点是南方城市杭州。

九曲黄河（时代图片供）

Scholar's Rocks

Rock appreciation has a long history in China. The ornamental rocks range in size from miniatures of a few inches high to those larger than human size. Huge prized rocks were placed in gardens, as called garden rocks. The beautiful and elaborate gardens of Suzhou, for example, contained such prized rocks, many of which were of elegant shapes and served as objects of contemplation. Small favored rocks were taken into a scholar's study and were referred to as scholar's rocks, and certain small rocks were placed on a desk to be brushrests, or made inkstones and **seals**, etc.

The commonest scholar's rocks are made of mostly limestone, which are often found in caves that have been eroded by underground streams. Scholar's rocks differ from garden rocks in exhibiting a higher degree of complex interior and surfaces. They are also placed on carved wooden stands that elevate them and complement their unique forms. The literati class that collected beautiful and interesting rock specimens into their studies believed that Nature engaged in creating art in producing such strange and evocative forms.

供石

Like landscape painting, scholar's rocks reflect the universe in microcosm, providing the scholar with a stimulus to meditation on nature while remaining in the confines of his study. The rocks' abstract qualities appealed to Chinese scholar aesthetes, much in the way that abstract sculpture might appeal to a western aesthete today.

供　石

中国的赏石文化历史悠久。观赏石大小不一，从仅数英寸高的微型石到比人还高的巨石都有。形体巨大的珍奇异石被安置在花园中供人观赏，称为园石。例如，苏州的那些美丽而精巧的园林里就有这种珍奇异石，很多奇石姿态美妙，引人遐想。形体较小的受人喜爱的奇石被摆放在书房里，称为供石。也有些小石头被放置在书桌上当作笔架，或制成砚台和**印章**等。

最常见的供石质地主要是石灰石，常发现于受地下水冲刷的洞穴中。供石与园石不同，供石的内部和表面更复杂。供石也会被放置在雕花的木质底座上，底座会将其抬高，以彰显其独特造型。在书房中收藏美丽有趣供石的文人们相信，是大自然的鬼斧神工创造了如此奇异而生动的艺术造型。

供石就像山水画，是整个宇宙的缩影，为学者们提供了足不出户，却能对自然进行沉思冥想的机会。这些石头的抽象品质吸引中国士大夫美学家，就如同抽象雕塑吸引今天的西方美学家。

供石

Seals

Seals in China, which date back some 4 000 years, were used for two main purposes: (1) to seal or close a letter or document; (2) to mark one's possessions to identify ownership and thus prevent theft. After unifying China, **Emperor** Qin Shi Huang had a seal made for himself from a valuable piece of jade. Seals were used by the nobility as a sign of their power. More functional seals were used by governmental administrators, while seals were also used by private individuals as a sign of their identity.

Affixing seals became common during the **Qin dynasty** (221 BC –

206 BC), when people engraved their names on documents to indicate authorship and on everyday household objects as a sign of ownership. The use of seals reached a zenith during the **Ming** (1368 – 1644) and **Qing dynasties** (1616 – 1911), when artists stamped their paintings with seal as both a signature and a way to increase their visual interest. Along with calligraphy, painting, and poetry, the cutting of seals is considered one of the four arts expected of the Chinese scholar. Seals reflect deep Chinese cultural roots and combine qualities of calligraphy and engraving, which has led to their being valued as works of art as well as functional objects for everyday and official use.

As works of art, seals are examined for their composition, their calligraphy, and the engraver's artful handwork in its effects of vigor and grace. Like **calligraphy**, seals, moreover, reflect a person's individual distinctiveness in taste and character.

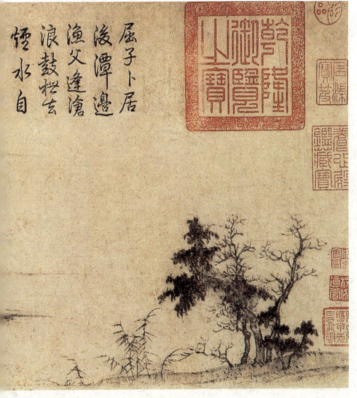

中国书画上都盖有印章

印　章

中国印·舞动的北京
（2008北京奥运会会徽）

中国的印章大约出现在四千年前，主要有两个用途：一是用来在书信或文件上署名，二是标记物品归属，防止盗窃。秦始皇统一中国后，用一块珍贵的玉为自己制作了一枚印章。贵族用印章作为一种权力符号，朝廷大臣用印章行使多种功能，私人用印章表明身份。

秦朝（前221—前206），加盖印章变得常见起来。人们将名字印在文件上以标明作者，印在日常生活用品上以标明所有者。**明**（1368—1644）**清**（1616—1911）时期，印章的使用达到顶峰。画家

在绘画作品上加盖印章，既是画家的签名，又增加画面的美感。印章的篆刻与书法、绘画和作诗一起，被视为中国文人应该掌握的四门艺术。印章折射了中国文化的深厚底蕴，结合了书法艺术和篆

明·何震《延赏楼印》（徽州文化博物馆供）

刻技巧，既是珍贵的艺术品，又是日常和办公用品。

　　作为艺术品，印章的好坏看其构图、书法和篆刻者的刀法，能否显出优雅而具活力的效果。此外，印章与**书法**一样，也反映个人的独特品位和性格。

古代的印章

Silk

Fine silk has long been appreciated in China for its richness of color, its light and soft texture, and its beauty. It is a mysterious product that derives from the spinning of the silkworm, whose lifespan of just four weeks is spent spinning around 3 300 feet of silk thread. A man's silk tie consumes the silk from more than 100 cocoons. Another way of quantifying is to note that an average cocoon contains about 0.35 gram of silk, that it takes 5 000 silkworms to produce two pounds of raw silk and that one ounce of eggs produces 20 000 silkworms, which consume a ton of mulberry leaves during their silk spinning month of life.

Silk was produced as early as over 5 000 years ago, with silk production peaking during the **Han dynasty** (206 BC – AD 220), when silk was transported from Chang'an (present day **Xi'an**) all the way to Rome. It was the so-called "silk road" or "silk route" that connected China to the rest of the world. In fact, there were at least two main routes, one by land, the other by sea. The land route started from Chang'an, going west across deserts and over mountains through certain central and western Asian countries and finally reaching Europe. The sea route started from the coastal cities in southern China, where silk would be carried by boat to southeast Asian countries like Vietnam, Thailand and Burma, and then onto India and further west until it reached Rome via the Mediterranean, from whence it was transported to other European capitals.

Legend holds that it was Luo Zu, the wife of the legendary Yellow Emperor (one of the two alleged ancestors of all Chinese), that invented raising silkworms, reeling off raw silk from cocoons and weaving silk. Since deified, she has been worshipped as the goddess of silkworms. Silk has been used for clothing, for surfaces for painting and calligraphy, as material for draperies and furniture coverings, for navigational charts, typewriter ribbons, insulation of spaceships, for various kinds of decoration and lining, including the lining of caskets, etc.

丝　绸

做蚕丝被用的丝絮（毛尧泉摄影）

在中国，精美的丝绸因其色彩鲜艳、质地轻软、图案美丽而长期受人喜爱。丝绸是用蚕吐的丝制成的一种神奇的纺织品。蚕的一生虽然只有四周，却会吐出约 3 300 英尺的蚕丝，制作一条男士丝绸领带需要消耗一百多个蚕茧的丝。换种方式计算，平均每个蚕茧约有 0.35 克丝，生产两磅生丝共需五千只蚕。每盎司蚕卵可孵出两万只蚕，这些蚕在吐丝阶段的一个月里将消耗一吨重的桑叶。

丝绸的生产早在五千多年前就开始了，到**汉朝**（前 206 — 220）达到顶峰，当时丝绸从长安（今天的**西安**）一直运到罗马。是所谓"丝绸之路"把中国和世界连接了起来。事实上，丝绸之路有至少两条主要路线，一条是陆路，一条是海路。陆路从长安开始，向西穿过沙漠，翻越大山，经过中亚和西亚的一些国家，最后到达欧洲。海路从中国南方沿海城市开始，那里的丝绸先用船运到东南亚的越南、泰国、缅甸等国，然后继续到印度，再西行经地中海到罗马，从那里运往欧洲其他国家的首都。

丝绸旗袍

据传说，是黄帝的妻子螺祖发明的养蚕、抽丝，织丝为绸，螺祖后来被尊为蚕神。丝绸用于制衣、书画、帐幔和家具罩、航海图、打字机色带、太空船绝缘设备、各种装饰和衬里，包括首饰盒的衬里等。

Song Dynasty

The Song dynasty (960 – 1279) established a reunified China after more than fifty years of division and chaos following the fall of the **Tang dynasty** in 907. Among the most brilliant of Chinese dynasties, the Song was a time of significant social and economic change, and a period that influenced the political and intellectual future of the country.

During the first half of the Song dynasty (960 – 1127), the capital was located in Bianliang (modern Kaifeng), and is known as the Northern Song dynasty. During the second half of the Song dynasty (1127 – 1279), the capital was located in Hangzhou, south of the **Yangtze** River. Some time during the early part of the Song dynasty, a political shift took place in which a central bureaucracy of scholars who won their positions through examinations administered the country instead of rule by a hereditary aristocracy.

Among best known cultural creations of the Northern Song dynasty are its landscape paintings. With the country in turmoil with the overthrow of the Tang **emperors**, painters retreated to the **mountains** for safety and seclusion, discovering in nature the serenity and moral order that was lacking in society. The Song artists envisioned the mountains in their landscapes as great rulers among their subjects. Song emperors, especially Huizong (reigned 1101 – 1125), who was an accomplished calligrapher and painter, provided support and encouragement to landscape painters, and recruited painters for the court and trained them in what became a highly realistic Song dynastic style. This style, however, was rejected by Neo-Confucian scholars, who had come to assume an important role in civil administration of the country, for a style that valued greater spontaneity and individual expression.

宋　朝

公元 907 年**唐朝**灭亡后，中国经历了 50 多年的分裂与混乱，最后由宋朝（960 — 1279）再度统一。宋朝是中国最辉煌的朝代之一，经历了重大的社会和经济变革，对后世的政治和思想产生了深远影响。

宋朝的第一个时期称为北宋（960 — 1127），国都在汴梁（即现在的开封）；第二个时期称为南宋（1127 — 1279），国都在**长江**以南的杭州。北宋时期，政治上进行了改革，一批通过考试进入中央官僚体系的学者接替世袭贵族管理国家。

北宋最著名的文化产物之一是山水画。在唐朝统治被推翻后，社会陷入一片混乱，画家们纷纷归隐山

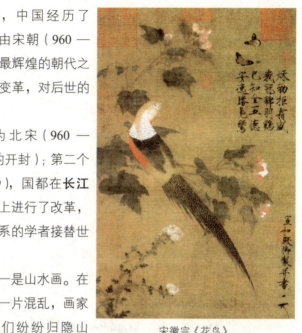

宋徽宗《花鸟》

林，在自然界中发现了社会生活所缺乏的宁静和道德秩序。宋代画家视笔下的高山为最伟大的主题。宋朝**皇帝**，特别是书画大家宋徽宗（1101 — 1125 年在位），为山水画家提供帮助和鼓励，并将画家召入宫廷加以培养，促进了宋代高度写实的宫廷画风的形成。然而，这一画风被后来在治理国家方面发挥重要作用的新儒家学者所摒弃，他们推崇尚写意和个人表现的画风。

宋徽宗像

Spring Festival (Chinese New Year)

S pring Festival, the Lunar New Year, is the most important holiday of the Chinese calendar. Celebrated throughout China, Spring Festival, or the Lunar New Year, celebrates the return of spring and its renewal of energy and life after the dark, cold, spell of winter. The Lunar New Year celebrates the spring's **Yang** after the winter's **Yin**.

During Spring Festival celebration, families travel all over the vast country to be with one another. Families celebrate the end of the old year and the beginning of the new, symbolized by such things as the repaying of debts and the settlement of disputes. On the eve of the Lunar New Year, the entire family gets together for a feast. Family members who have died are also provided with a place, so as to include them in spirit.

Spring Festival traditionally lasts up to two weeks and concludes with the colorful lantern festival. For the national legal holidays of the eve and the first six days of the Chinese Lunar Year, known as the golden week of Spring Festival, no one works. In the modern world, however, business people are connected through their mobile phones or email accounts, accessible via the Internet. But many people still retain prohibitions against work as to interfering with the luck of the New Year. The final night of the two-week festival, Lantern Festival, is celebrated with lanterns as it marks the first full moon of the New Year. Street entertainers abound to provide joy for the crowds of celebrants.

春节（中国新年）

　　春节是中国日历里最重要的节假日。春节即阴历新年，是全中国人民共同庆祝的节日。它象征着在黑暗、寒冷的冬天之后春天的归来、能量的恢复和生命的复苏，并庆祝春天的**阳**取代了冬天的**阴**。

　　春节期间，家庭成员会从各地千里迢迢赶回家中团聚，家家户户庆祝旧的一年的结束和新的一年的开始，并以还清债务、解决纠纷等作为除旧迎新的象征。除夕之夜，全家人会坐在一起共享团圆饭。他们给去世的家庭成员留出席位，以便其灵魂与他们一起共贺新春。

　　传统上，春节的庆祝活动持续长达两周，并以热闹而多彩的元宵节作为结束。除夕至正月初六是国家法定假日，称为春节黄金周，人们都不工作。然而，现在的工商业者会借助手机或互联网的电子邮箱联络、谈生意。不过，很多人还是坚持不工作，认为此时工作会影响新的一年的运气。在两周节庆的最后一夜元宵节，人们点起灯笼，庆祝新年的第一轮满月。街头的众多艺人为庆祝的人群带来欢乐。

春节（时代图片供）

Tai Chi Chuan

Tai Chi Chuan, is most commonly practiced today in China as a form of exercise, though, historically, it has also been a type of **Kung Fu**, considered one of the martial arts. Followers and practitioners around the world, and especially in China, typically perform Tai Chi Chuan for its health benefits, both physical and mental. Throughout China, in villages and cities, in parks and other public spaces, people practice their Tai Chi Chuan slow motion exercises.

Tai Chi Chuan promotes a focusing of attention on one's body, creating greater bodily awareness, with a particular emphasis on balance both physical and mental. Other benefits include improved flexibility and cardiovascular fitness. Tai Chi Chuan training also helps practitioners develop a greater appreciation for moderation and self-control.

A major goal of Tai Chi Chuan for health maintenance is to enable practitioners to reduce tension and stress through increasing circulation of blood and breath to improve bodily functions. Through relieving stress and reducing tension, practitioners increase their energy and consolidate their strength for use in pursuing their careers, hobbies, and family lives. The control of body and mind achieved through Tai Chi Chuan also serves as a necessary preparation for further meditation practice or other martial arts training.

太 极 拳

太极拳今天在中国主要被当作一种健身运动，不过在历史上，它也是一种**功夫**，是一种重要的武术门类。在全世界，特别是在中国，太极拳爱好者和练习者通常通过练习太极拳保持身心健康。在中国各地，无论农村还是城市，公园或是其他公共场所，都有人在慢悠悠地打太极拳。

太极拳特别强调身心的平衡，它有助于加强练习者对自身的专注，提高身体意识，并能改善身体的柔韧性、维护心血管健康。太极拳还能帮助练习者培养沉稳的品质和自我控制的能力。

太极拳强身健体的一个主要目的就是通过增加气血的流通以改进身体功能，缓解紧张，减轻压力。一旦紧张得到缓解，压力得到减轻，练习者的气就会增加，力量就会增强，从而更好地追求自己的事业、业余爱好和家庭生活。通过练习太极拳所取得的对精神和身体的控制还可以作为进一步修行或习练其他武术的必要准备。

太极拳（时代图片供）

Tang Dynasty

The Tang dynasty (618 – 907) was one of the most peaceful and artistically fruitful in Chinese history. The foundation for the prosperity and the accomplishments of the Tang dynasty was laid by their predecessors of the Sui, who ruled from 581 to 618, and who had reunified China and reestablished order after 270 years of division, war and turmoil during the Southern and Northern dynasties. During the Tang dynasty, far-reaching diplomacy and implementation of benevolent rule coupled with economic expansion to create an efflorescence of culture, to make it one of the world's greatest empires.

The Tang capital was at Chang'an, **Xi'an** today, then the most populous city in the world, and one where foreigners from Persia and Arabia, India and Syria, the Korean Peninsula and Japan thronged the streets. The zenith of the Tang dynasty was the eighth century, considered the golden age of Chinese literature and art, when craftsmen created a remarkable array of glazed ceramic porcelain in the form of marvelously realistic camels, horses, graceful courtesans, and fierce tomb guardians.

Many Tang dynasty poets have a high reputation in the history of Chinese literature and wide recognition in the world. The court painter Wu Daozi (690 – 760), the poet, painter and musician Wang Wei (699 – 759), and the poets **Li Bai** (701 – 762) and **Du Fu** (712 – 770) set the standard for artistic excellence for future generations.

During the Tang dynasty, landscape painting was the most important genre. Called *shanshui* (**mountain**-water), Tang landscape paintings were simple and austere, designed not to portray nature exactly but to convey its spirit and rhythms. Considerable development was also achieved in music during the Tang dynasty especially the *qin,* or **bamboo** flute, and **opera** undergone great innovation in way of performance, which was performed for the pleasure of **Emperor** Xuanzong (712 – 755), who founded the first opera troupe in China.

唐 朝

唐朝（618 — 907）是中国历史上社会最安定、艺术成就最辉煌的时期之一。唐朝繁荣和成就的基础是之前的隋朝（581 — 618）奠定的，隋朝结束了南北朝270年的分裂与战乱，重新统一了中国，重建了社会秩序。唐代，外交广泛，施行仁政，再加上经济发展，造就了一个文化鼎盛的时期，使唐朝成为世界上最伟大的帝国之一。

唐朝定都长安（即现在的**西安**）。长安是当时世界上人口最多的城市，街道上满是来自波斯和阿拉伯、印度和叙利亚、朝鲜半岛和日本的外国人。公元8世纪是唐朝的鼎盛时期，被视为中国文学和艺术的黄金时期。当时，工匠烧制了形形色色的彩釉陶瓷器，称为"唐三彩"，这些艺术品包括非常逼真的骆驼、马、姿态幽雅的侍女以及形象凶猛的镇墓兽。

许多唐代诗人不仅在中国文学史上享有盛名，而且得到世界公认。宫廷画师吴道子（约690 —760），同时身为诗人、画家和音乐家的王维（699 —759）、诗人**李白**（701 —762）和**杜甫**（712 —770）都是后人心目中最优秀的艺术家或诗人。

在唐代，风景画（称为**山水画**）是最重要的画种，画面简明朴实，目的不是对自然进行仔细临摹，而是更注重表达自然的灵动和韵律。唐代音乐也获得了极大的发展，特别是琴、**竹**笛和**戏剧**的表演形式发生了巨大的变革。玄宗**皇帝**（712—755）喜好戏剧表演，并成立了中国第一个剧团。

唐·王维《长江积雪图》局部

Tea

Tea culture in China has a four-thousand-year history. It was among the tributes the state of Ba paid to King Wu of Zhou when King Wu launched an expedition against King Zhou of the Shang dynasty (1046 BC). It wasn't until the **Tang dynasty** that it became a popular drink. Tea spread from China to other Asian countries, especially Japan in the sixth century. It was carried then to other parts of the world, including Africa and Europe in the seventeenth century, and on to America in the eighteenth century.

Tea is consumed by more people than any other beverages, including coffee and cocoa, with green tea (especially *longjing* tea) the most popular variety. At once a pacifying drink and a stimulating one, tea offers spiritual as well as physical benefits. Physically, tea drinking aids digestion, stimulates metabolic activity, and acts as an anti-inflammatory. Socially, it lubricates conversations, relaxes people, easing tension and reducing anxiety.

Unlike Japan, where the tea culture emphasizes the ceremonies and utensils associated with tea, in China, the tea itself is the most important element of its tea culture. The Chinese take their tea so seriously that, if when dining out, the tea is not brewed properly, it will be sent back, much like in the West, where an unsatisfactory bottle of wine may be rejected.

红茶制作手册（徽州文化博物馆供）

茶

　　茶文化在中国已有至少四千年历史，周武王伐纣时（前 1046）巴国给周武王的贡品中就有茶。不过，直到**唐朝**茶才成为一种流行饮料。茶从中国流传到了其他亚洲国家，特别是在 6 世纪传到日本，又在 17 世纪传到非洲和欧洲，18 世纪传到美洲。

　　喝茶的人比喝任何其他饮料（包括咖啡和可可）的人都多，绿茶，特别是龙井茶，最受欢迎。茶既有镇静功效，又能提神，对身体和精神都有好处。从身体角度看，饮茶有助于消化、刺激新陈代谢，并具有消炎作用。从社交角度看，茶有助于谈话顺利进行，帮助人们放松，减轻紧张和焦虑感。

　　中国人喝茶与日本人不同。在日本，茶文化讲究与茶有关的仪式和器皿；在中国，茶本身就是茶文化最重要的成分。中国人对茶非常看重。在外就餐时，如果茶沏得不好，他们会要求退掉，就像西方人不接受不好的葡萄酒一样。

茶

Umbrellas

Umbrellas in China date back more than four thousand years, with the earliest ones made of silk, followed by umbrellas made of paper, which were processed with tung oil to repel water. Umbrella frames were often made of bamboo because it is both light and strong. Yellow umbrellas used to be used only by members of the royal family.

The word *umbrella* derives from a Latin word, *umbra*, which means "shade" or "shadow". The Chinese character for umbrella 伞 is a pictograph resembling the shape of an umbrella. The umbrella's primary purpose was to ward off sun or rain, to shade its holder from the elements of heat or water. And though umbrellas originated in China, they became popular throughout the world, but especially in northern European countries with wet climates. In fact, the first shop devoted exclusively to umbrellas was that of James Smith and Sons, in London, which opened in 1830.

The best traditional Chinese umbrellas are believed to be those made in Fujian Province, where umbrella ribs for the frame are made from five-year-old bamboo, which can be made resistant to moisture, mold, and insects. The most beautiful umbrellas are widely thought to be those of Hangzhou. Fine Chinese umbrellas involve more than eighty different steps in processing their five main parts: the ribs, shaft, head, umbrella cover, and decorative painting.

Umbrellas in China today are made of various materials, including cotton, silk, nylon, oil paper, and plastic film. Apart from preventing people from sunshine and rain, umbrellas are used as props by actors on stage, like the high wire artist, who uses the umbrella for balance.

伞

四千多年前，伞就已经在中国出现。最早的伞用丝帛制成，后有纸伞，用上过桐油的防水纸制成。伞架多用竹制成，因为竹轻而坚韧。在过去，黄色的伞只有皇族才能使用。

伞的英语 umbrella 源自拉丁文 umbra，意为阴影或影子。汉字"伞"是个象形字，表现伞的外形。伞的基本功能是遮光挡雨，使打伞人免遭日晒雨淋。伞尽管是中国发明的，却在世界范围内流行开来，特别是在气候潮湿的北欧国家。事实上，第一家专门售伞的商店是 1830 年在伦敦开业的 James Smith & Sons。

据称，中国最好的传统伞产自福建，其伞骨用生长五年的竹子制成，可防潮、防霉、防虫蛀。最漂亮的伞公认是杭州生产的。制作一把精致的中国伞共有八十多道工序，加工五个主要部件：伞骨、伞柄、伞头、伞面和彩绘。

现在，中国的伞有多种材料，包括棉、绸、尼龙、油纸和塑料膜。伞除了供人们遮阳挡雨，还被演员作为演出时的道具，如走钢丝的杂技演员用伞来保持身体平衡。

旅游景点售卖的传统工艺伞

Virtues

A longstanding traditional value in Chinese culture is the extent to which one's status is determined by one's virtue rather than by one's wealth or one's birth. The word for virtue in Chinese is "te", a critically important concept in Confucianism and in **Daoism**.

The sayings of **Confucius** and the writings of **Laotze** are replete with discussion of virtuous living. Among the Confucian virtues are *jen*, or benevolence and compassion; *yi*, or righteousness and sense of duty; *li*, or rites and propriety; *zhi*, or knowledge and wisdom; and *xin*, or honesty and trustworthiness. Among the Daoist virtues are humility, tolerance, simplicity, spontaneity, and integrity. All of these principles of virtues have become cultural signposts and markers for what is most important to Chinese people past and present.

To Confucian scholars, what holds all the virtues together – the central concept that governs all virtue – is propriety, behaving towards others in acceptably appropriate ways based on proper attitudes and guided by respect. And when propriety is observed, right action and right thought are in evidence, with the result that relationships are in harmony, a quality that strengthens individuals as well as social groups.

美　德

中国文化的一个历史悠久的价值取向是，一个人的地位是由其德而不是由其财富或出身决定的。德即品德和德行，是儒家和**道家**学说中一个至关重要的概念。

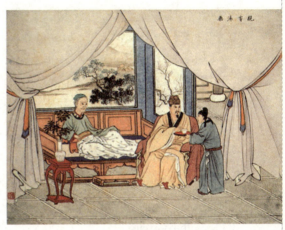

孔子的教诲和**老子**的文章中充满对品德和德行的讨论。儒家所说的德包括仁、义、礼、智、信。道家的德包括谦卑、容忍、纯朴、率真、诚信。所有这些关于"德"的信条已成为古往今来中国人眼中最重要的文化路标和标志。

亲尝汤药

对于儒家学者来说，所有这些美德都围绕一个中心——礼，即一个人在言行举止上对待他人须采取可接受的恰当方式，态度要正确，要待人以礼。人人若守礼，就会有正确的行动和思想，就会实现社会关系的和谐，这种和谐又将增强个人和社会群体的力量。

"礼"是中国人的座右铭

Warriors

To people outside of China, the best known Chinese warriors are the terracotta warriors of the mausoleum of the first **Qin dynasty** (220 BC – 206 BC) **Emperor**. Found near the mausoleum of Emperor Qin Shi Huang, more than 8 000 figures, including soldiers, horses, chariots, weapons, and other military accoutrements have been found, with continued digging yielding many more. As one of the most important archeological finds of the twentieth century, discoveries of the terracotta warriors near the city of **Xi'an** have been made over a period of more than thirty years.

Because the material out of which the life-size figures are made, terracotta, or baked earth, is fragile, many figures have had to be reconstructed from fragments. Originally, terracotta warriors were anything but dull looking, as they were glazed with a lacquer finish and painted various colors, though few of the figures have retained much of that coloring now.

One of the remarkable things about the terracotta warriors is that they are not identical, each possessing its own distinctive features. The figures include infantrymen, archers, and officers, some standing and others crouching. Originally, they carried various kinds of weapons, including swords, spears, and wooden crossbows. The Museum in which the figures can now be seen includes arrangements of men and horses in battle formations to exhibit the appearance of the national troops in the Qin dynasty.

武　士

　　对于中国以外的人来说，中国最著名的武士是秦始皇陵的兵马俑。兵马俑发掘于秦始皇陵附近，已经发掘出八千余件，包括兵俑、马俑、战车、兵器和其他军事装备。兵马俑是 20 世纪最重要的考古发现之一，发掘工作在**西安**附近进行，至今已持续三十余年，现在仍在进行。

　　制作这些实物大小的俑所用的材料是经烧制的陶土，由于陶易碎，许多俑已经破成碎片，现在只好将这些碎片重新组合起来。兵马俑原先完全不是现在这种灰暗的颜色，而是曾被刷上油漆，涂上各种颜色。不过，现在身上仍有颜色的兵马俑极其稀少。

　　特别值得一提的是，兵马俑中没有两个完全一样的陶俑，它们各有特点。兵俑包括步兵、弓箭手和军官，或立或半跪。他们原先持有各种武器，如剑、矛、木弩等。在陈列兵马俑的博物馆里，兵俑和马俑被排列成作战阵形，展现了当年秦国军队的气派。

武士俑

兵马俑博物馆

Xi'an

Thirteen Chinese dynasties had their capital in Xi'an, formerly called Chang'an. The earliest was the western **Zhou dynasty** in the eleventh through eighth centuries BC. The last was the **Tang dynasty** (618 – 907). The most famous dynasty to make Xi'an its capital was the **Qin dynasty** (221 BC – 206 BC), because near the Mausoleum of the first Qin **Emperor**, Qin Shi Huang, thousands of terracotta **warriors** with horses and weapons were excavated. With more than 3 000 years of history and a location as the eastern end of the ancient **Silk** Road, it is one of the most important cities and cultural centers in Chinese history, and it remains an important center of Chinese cultural life.

Located in a fertile area with a plentiful water supply, and militarily formidable because of the **mountains** that nearly surround it, Xi'an has been China's historical center for hundreds of years. Actions occurring in Xi'an reverberated for thousands of miles throughout the country. Ancient laws were inscribed on stone tablets and ancient rites accompanied by music were created in Xi'an during the Zhou dynasty. It was in Xi'an, too, that the Qin dynasty which unified the country, and established a centralized society. And it was in Xi'an that the **Han** and **Tang dynasties** located their capitals, then called Chang'an. One can't travel far on the outskirts of Xi'an without coming across layers of Chinese history in the form of relics of these ancient dynasties.

Today Xi'an is a thriving metropolis and the most important city in the northwest of China. Its residents continue to balance past and present, the ancient world and its culture and traditions, with globalization and modernity.

西　安

　　西安古称长安，是中国历史上 13 个朝代的都城。公元前 11 世纪至公元前 8 世纪的西**周**是在此定都的第一个王朝，**唐朝**（618 — 907）是最后一个。最著名的定都西安的王朝是**秦朝**（前 221 — 前 206），因为在秦朝的第一位**皇帝**秦始皇的陵墓附近出土了数以千计的兵马俑和武器。西安有三千多年历史，是古**丝绸**之路的东方起点。它是中国历史上最重要的城市和文化中心之一，至今仍是中国文化生活的一个重要中心。

　　西安土地肥沃、水源充足，几乎被群**山**环抱，军事上易守难攻。千百年来，西安一直是中国历史上的中心城市。西安发生的事件会波及数千英里外，影响全国。周朝时，西安有篆刻在石碑上的古代法规，有带音乐伴奏的古代典礼。同样在西安，统一了全国的秦朝，建立了中央集权的社会。**汉朝**和**唐朝**也定都于此，当时称为"长安"。在西安城郊，走不远就能看到这些朝代的遗迹，它们是中国历史的积淀。

　　今天的西安是一个蓬勃发展的大都市，是中国西北部最重要的城市。西安人在继续维护着过去和现在之间的平衡，维护着古代文化传统和全球化、现代化之间的平衡。

西安车展（时代图片供）

Yangtze

The Yangtze is China's longest **river**, the longest river in Asia, and the third largest river in the world after the Nile in Africa and the Amazon in South America. It used to be called simply the *Jiang*, which means "river", and the section below Yangzhou was referred to as the *Yangtze Jiang*. Its modern name in Chinese, *Chang Jiang*, means "Long River", an apt designation for the longest river in China that flows for more than 6 200 kilometers (3 860 miles). The Yangtze River flows through three dramatic gorges, with stunning natural scenery: the Qutang Gorge, Wu Gorge, and Xiling Gorge. Together these are known as the *San Xia*, or Three Gorges.

Traditionally, but unofficially, the Yangtze River, which flows from west to east, has been considered the geo-political dividing line between the northern and southern parts of China because of the difficulty of crossing its waters. Along its circuitous route, the Yangtze receives waters from thousands of tributaries and lakes and finally reaches its end in the East China Sea at Shanghai.

Historically, the Yangtze is important as the center of ancient Chinese cultural origins, with humans being active in the area of the Three Gorges from about two million years ago. Important cities have been located for centuries along its banks, including Chongqing, Wuhan, Shanghai, etc. During the **Han dynasty** (206 BC – AD 220), the Yangtze increased in economic importance and during the **Qing dynasty** (1616 – 1911), half of the country's revenues were derived from cities along its flowing route.

Today the river has been a center of hot debate, with the Three Gorges Dam arguably making the traditional flooding of its banks worse. Others contend that the dam will improve the lives of people along the river by providing them with electricity and the benefits that accrue from it.

长 江

长江是中国和亚洲最长的**河流**，位居世界第三，仅次于非洲的尼罗河和南美的亚马孙河。长江过去叫"江"，扬州以下的河段叫"扬子江"，西方至今仍多称之为"扬子江"（the Yangtze River）。后来之所以叫长江，是因为它有 6 200 多公里长，是中国最长的河流。长江流经三个风景如画的峡谷：瞿塘峡、巫峡、西陵峡，合称为"三峡"。

长江自西向东流淌，难以横渡，从而在地理政治上将中国分为南北两大区域。长江迂回蜿蜒，途中汇入数千支流和湖泊的水，最终在上海流入东海。

长江具有重要的历史意义，是中国古文化发祥地之一；早在两百万年前，三峡地区就有人类活动。长江沿岸千百年来一直分布着一些重要城市，包括重庆、武汉和上海等。**汉朝**（前 206 —220 ），长江在经济上变得更重要了，在**清朝**（1616 —1911 ），国家收入的一半来自于沿江城市。

如今，人们围绕这条河上的三峡大坝展开了激烈辩论。有人论证说，大坝会加剧沿岸的洪涝灾害。其他人则认为，大坝可以发电，并带来其他效益，有助于提高两岸居民的生活水平。

巫峡画廊（时代图片供）

YinYang

One of the best known of all Chinese images is that of the Yin and Yang. Yin and Yang together represent contrasting but complementary principles that sum up life's basic opposing elements – pain and pleasure, good and evil, male and female, light and dark. Instead of seeing Yin and Yang as contradictory, the Chinese emphasize the ways these opposites interact to mutually support and reinforce one another.

Yin and Yang illustrate the philosophical ideal of harmonious integration of opposites. In the Yin Yang symbol, they coexist peacefully within a larger circle. Each form, Yin and Yang provides the border for its opposite, partly defining it. In the very center of each form, there is the defining aspect of the complementary other. The dark teardrop contains a spot of white; the white teardrop includes a small dark circle.

Yin represents the negative forms, associated with the earth, darkness, and passivity. Yang represents the positive form and is associated with heaven, light, and the constructive impulse. Together, Yin and Yang represent the perpetual interplay and mutual relation of all things. Everything that exists consists of Yin and Yang in varying proportions. In their combined complementarity, Yin and Yang embody the ancient view of the cosmos, in which everything that exists on earth and beyond is constituted of a single vital principle or substance called *Qi* (Chee). *Qi* manifests itself in the familiar Yin and Yang design of differing but complementary forces.

Ultimately, *Qi* and its ebb and flow in the Yin Yang pattern, represents a highly monistic view of existence. Everything that exists is related to everything else; all existence emerges from and presses toward a single essential substance.

阴 阳

　　中国最著名的图形之一是阴阳图。阴和阳体现了对立互补原理，总结了生活中的基本对立成分——痛苦和欢乐、善和恶、男和女、光明和黑暗。中国人并不将阴和阳视为冲突，而是重视对立双方的相互补充、相互作用和相互促进。

　　阴阳观念阐述了对立双方和谐统一的哲学理想。在阴阳图里，阴和阳在同一大圆中和平共存，各自为对方提供疆界，并一起界定这个图。各方中心区域均有对方标记，黑水滴区里有一白点，白水滴区里有一黑点。表示阳中有阴，阴中有阳，双方相辅相成。

　　阴代表消极的一面，与地、黑暗和被动相联系。阳代表积极的一面，与天、光明和主动有关。阴阳共同体现了万物永远此消彼长、相互作用的关系。万物皆有阴阳，只是比例有所不同。互补的阴阳体现了古人的宇宙观。古人认为，地球和宇宙万物都由一种叫做"气"的唯一生命法则或物质构成。气的表现形式就是我们所熟悉的、由不同但互补的力量组成的阴阳图。

阴阳图

　　气及其阴阳消长从根本上体现了高度的一元论存在观。万物间皆有联系，万物皆生于同一物质，并终将归于该物质。

173

Zen

Zen is a system of philosophy and spirituality developed in India, transported to China in the sixth century, and then a few centuries later to a number of other East Asian countries, where it flourished as a type of **Buddhism**. Zen also became a major religious and cultural force, with a strong aesthetics evident in poetry, painting, and the tea ceremony. In China, Zen, or "Ch'an", from the Sanscrit word *dhyana*, meaning "meditation", blended with thoughts of **Laotze** and Chuangtze, with the mystic experience of Buddhist enlightenment merging with the profound ideas of the *Daodejing* and Chuangtze's state of forgetting the world and ones' ego, to get a new development.

Zen has been described as the art of seeing into one's own nature or being. Although often defined as a religion or a philosophy, Zen is more accurately described as a way of living, an emphatically active stance toward everyday experience. With an emphasis on the present, Zen focuses on experiencing the moment in all its fullness of being. It encourages followers to savor each experience, whatever it involves, whether meditating, eating or drinking, walking or standing still, working or playing. It is concerned with the here and now, not with the afterlife. In Zen, one accepts life for what it is and what it brings. Life is to live in the moment, attentively and appreciatively.

Various Zen practices, most famously *zazen*, or seated meditation, can help practitioners reach the state where they can live in the present, and in which they can accept every eventuality with poise and equanimity. Zen *koans,* or riddles, aid in the process, as exemplified by the famous *koan* which says White Master Huineng, the sixth Patriarch of Zen Buddhism was taking over the mantle, he argued against Shenziu (a competitor for the mantle) on his perceptions of Zen as follows:

There is no Buddhist tree at all,
And there is bright mirror not.
Now there is nothing at all,
How could be dust any more?

西湖禅意（朱　绛摄影）

禅

宋·梁楷《六祖斫竹图》

禅是一种哲学和精神体系，源于印度，6世纪传到中国，几个世纪后传到日本和其他一些东亚国家，在这些国家作为**佛教**的一个派别而兴旺发达起来，成为一支主要的宗教和文化势力，其高超的审美观念在诗歌、绘画和茶道仪式中均有体现。"禅"是梵语"Dhyana"的音译，意思是"冥想"。在中国，禅与**老子**和庄子的思想相互交融，将佛教涅槃的神秘体验与《道德经》的玄妙思想以及庄子物我两忘的境界结合在一起获得了新的发展。

禅被形容为洞察人自身本质或存在的艺术。尽管它常被说成一种宗教或哲学，但更确切地说，它是一种生活方式，是积极面对生活体验的一种态度。禅讲究现在，关注对存在时刻的完全充分体验。它鼓励追随者享受每一时刻，不论是在做什么，不论是禅定、吃喝、行走或站立、工作或玩耍。它关心此时此刻，而不是来世。禅认为，生活不论是什么，不论带来什么，人们都应该接受它。生活就是以欣赏的眼光专心度过每一刻。

禅有多种修行方法，最著名的是参禅或打坐。这些修行方法能够帮助修行者进入入定的状态，使其平静、镇定地接受所有最终可能发生的事情。类似谜语的禅宗公案有助于这一过程。例如，一个著名的公案是禅宗六祖惠能在继承衣钵时与神秀关于禅的见解的争辩：

> 菩提本无树，
> 明镜亦非台。
> 本来无一物，
> 何处惹尘埃？

禅（朱　绛摄影）

Zhou Dynasty

The Zhou dynasty (1046 BC – 256 BC) which lasted for nearly eight hundred years, is the longest of the Chinese dynastic kingdoms. Believing himself to possess a Mandate from Heaven, King Wu of Zhou overthrew the Shang dynasty (1600 BC – 1046 BC) by defeating its ruler King Zhou (a homophone with the Zhou of the Zhou dynasty). The concept of the Mandate from Heaven, popular in the Shang dynasty and the Zhou dynasty, places the mandate or right to rule on the person who is morally worthy of such an august responsibility. Although the Zhou adopted many of the cultural practices of their predecessors, such as the Shang writing system, rituals, and administration, and inherited and refined the bronze arts of the Shang dynasty, they established a feudal system of governing. Land was distributed with landowners becoming vassals of the Zhou ruler, to whom they owed both homage and tribute, much as was done in the European Middle Ages.

The Zhou dynasty is divided into the Western Zhou (1046 BC – 771BC) and the Eastern Zhou (770 BC – 256 BC). This second half of the Zhou dynasty, the Eastern Zhou is itself traditionally divided into two parts: the Spring and Autumn Period (770 BC – 476 BC) and the Warring States Period (475 BC – 221 BC), during which the larger states contested for power of the entire country. In one of the ironies of Chinese history, it was during the Warring States Period that China experienced an efflorescence of classical philosophy. During this period, sometimes referred to as the One Hundred Schools Period, three influential philosophical systems developed: **Confucianism**, **Daoism**, and Legalism. The Zhou dynasty also included China's iron age, a time in which iron tools spurred the development of agriculture, which caused an explosion in the country's population.

周　朝

　　周朝（前1046 — 前256）有近八百年历史，是中国历史上最长的朝代。周武王认为自己具有天命，他打败商朝（前1600 — 前1046）的最后一位统治者纣王，推翻了商朝。 天命的概念在商周时期就已流行，这一概念认为，上天会将统治权降落在道德上能够担此重任的人身上。周朝沿袭了商朝的很多文化传统，如文字、祭祀和统治方法，继承和发展了商代的青铜艺术，但却建立了封建的统治制度。周朝将土地分给诸侯，诸侯必须效忠于周天子并敬献贡品，就像中世纪欧洲那样。

　　周朝分为西周（前1046 — 前771）和东周（前770 — 前256）。传统上，东周又被分为春秋（前770 — 前476）和战国时期（前475 — 前221）。这期间，大的诸侯国为争霸全国而征战。具有讽刺意味的是，中国的古典哲学在战国时期形成了鼎盛局面。这段时期又被称为百家争鸣的时期，出现了**儒家**、**道家**、法家三大哲学体系。周代，中国开始进入铁器时代，铁制工具的使用促进了农业的发展，刺激了人口的快速增长。

西周青铜器·保卣

Sources for Further Reading

推荐阅读资源

Readers who would like to learn more about various aspects of Chinese culture may wish to consult one or another of the following resources, which have proved helpful to the authors.

Arts and Culture: An Introduction to the Humanities, 3rd edition, Janetta Benton and Robert DiYanni, Prentice Hall

Book of Songs, translated by Arthur Waley, Grove Press

China: Customs and Etiquette, Kathy Flower, Graphic Arts Center Publishing

China: Empire and Civilization, edited by Edward L. Shaughnessy, Oxford University Press

Chinese Art, Mary Treager, Thames and Hudson

Confucianism, Jennifer Oldstone-Moore, Oxford University Press

Confucius, The Analects, translated by D. C. Lau, Penguin

Five Tang Poets, translated by David Young, Oberlin College Press

The Joy of Sects, Peter Occhiogrosso, Doubleday

Li Po (Bai) and Tu (Du) Fu: Poems, translated by Arthur Cooper, Penguin

Tao te Ching, translated by Stephen Mitchell, Random House

Daoism: The Way and its Power, translated by Holmes Welch

The World's Religions, Houston Smith, Harper Collins

Web Sites: chinapage.com; chinavista.com; chineseculture.net